DRIVING
THE
POWER GAME

DRIVING
THE
POWER GAME

CollinsWillow

An Imprint of HarperCollins*Publishers*

First published in 1993 by Collins Willow
an imprint of HarperCollins Publishers London

© SP Creative Design 1993

A CIP catalogue for this book is available from the British Library

ISBN 0 00 218 509-1

Designed and produced by
SP Creative Design
Linden House, Kings Road, Bury St Edmunds, Suffolk
Art Director: Rolando Ugolini
Editor: Heather Thomas
Production: Rolando Ugolini
Illustrations by Laurence Scarlett
Photographs by Rolando Ugolini, Mark Shearman and Yours in Sport

Typeset in Stone Serif by Halcyon Type & Design, Ipswich, Suffolk
Colour origination by J Film Process Company Ltd

Printed and bound in Italy by New Interlitho SpA, Milan

Acknowledgements
The publishers would like to thank the following:
John Murray (Publishers) Ltd for their kind permission to quote from
John Betjeman's *Seaside Golf* from his **Collected Poems.**
Arwyn Davies for appearing in some photographs.
Les Jones of Woodbridge Golf Club, Suffolk, for his help and advice.
The Sundridge Park Golf Club, Bromley, Kent, and Bob Cameron, the
Head Professional, for their help in photography.

Contents

Nick Allen

Nick Allen is a PGA professional and consultant with Apollo Golf Shafts, which operates a Tour Support Service on the European Tour.

Alasdair Barr

Alasdair Barr is the Director of Golf at Brocket Hall in Hertfordshire, England. He is also a Senior Swing Instructor and Examiner for the PGA Training School, and is National Coach to the English Golf Union and coaches the Berkshire, Buckinghamshire and Oxfordshire Senior, Junior and Ladies County teams.

Jim Christine

Jim Christine is the Golf Professional at Worplesdon Golf Club in Surrey, England. He is a Senior Swing Tutor with the PGA, and a regular contributor to *Golf World* magazine in the UK. He is also a member of *Golf World's* teaching panel and teaches at the *Golf World* schools.

Tony Moore

Tony Moore is the Head Golf Professional at St Mellion Golf Club in Cornwall, England. He coaches the County teams of both Devon and Cornwall and has taught several well-known golfers including Roger Winchester and Jonathan Langlead.

Driving

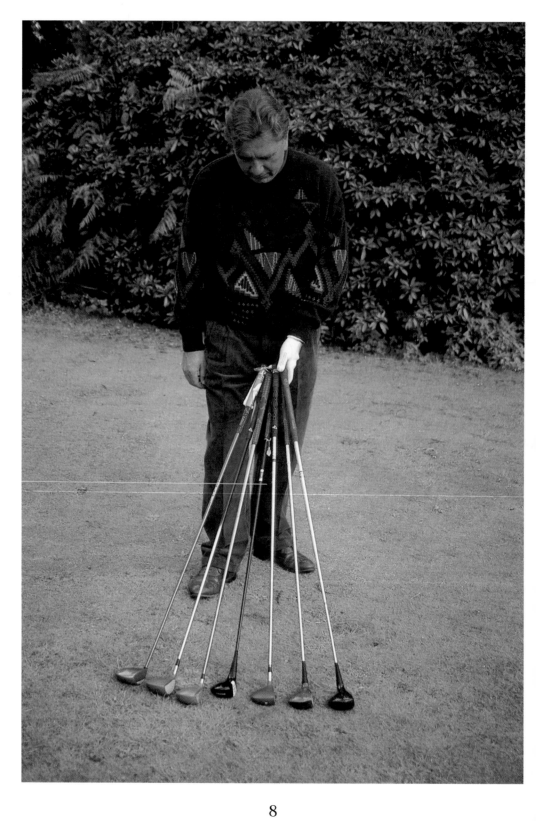

CHAPTER ONE

Equipment

Jim Christine

How straight it flew, how long it flew.
It clear'd the rutty track
And soaring, disappeared from view
Beyond the bunker's back -
A glorious, sailing, bounding drive
That made me glad I was alive.

(From **Seaside Golf** by Sir John Betjeman)

How well we can all identify with the sentiments expressed by John Betjeman. I am sure, however, we can all too easily remember the feelings we have when the opposite to that wonderful shot invades our game. The top, the scuff, the glorious feeling of a great strike dashed as we look up to see our ball sailing towards the out-of-bounds fence and finally into the field, housing estate or car park beyond. Our aim in the following pages is to help you play more drives akin to that outlined in the verse and resign the other horrors to only bad memories from the dim and distant past.

With a little practice in the right direction from you, I feel sure we can!

Equipment

The drive

The first question you should really ask is: "What is a drive?" Most people think that only those shots that are played with the driver, number 1 wood, are entitled to be called a drive. This is not so; the simple definition of a drive is that it is the first shot at each hole, the shot that puts the ball into play. It is on this point that I would like to start your learning process in becoming a successful driver of the ball. You have clearly not achieved your goal of putting the ball into play if you hit it out of bounds! I would also venture to suggest that if the ball lies in a bush, lake or river you will have great difficulty in playing your next shot from where the ball lies. You will probably need to take a penalty shot to get the ball into play, not a great start to any hole!

I hope you will understand from these opening remarks that it is far from correct just to think of your drive as an attempt to blast the ball as far as possible. In my experience this is the idea most people have in their heads as the definition of a drive, and it is this style of thinking that leads to all the problems players inevitably have with their drivers.

Of course, it is useful to be able to drive the ball a long way, but only if it stays on the golf course, in play for your next shot. Once you can keep it in play on most occasions, then the further you hit it the better; however, this is not the case every time, and indeed the driver is not always the club that will hit the ball furthest, as you will learn.

Let us go on to explore the world of drivers and driving the ball with a look at the tools of the trade.

The range of equipment

Originally, all drivers looked like the lovely old clubs we still see in museums and private collections. Persimmon heads, hickory shafts and hide grips were the order of the day, the main difference between them lying in the skill of the clubmaker. The choice was a very personal one.

Today this is still important, but the range of choice is vast, so big in fact that it can become a daunting task to the inexperienced. Worse still, it is all too easy to end up with a totally unsuitable club for your game. Metal heads, wooden heads; carbon shafts, steel shafts; mid-size, long-shafted, jumbo, high kick point, low kick point; it can be a minefield to the uninitiated. This chapter is dedicated to helping you understand the important areas of club technology and ultimately it should enable you to make sure that you are playing with the correct club.

Together we are going to look at what the club head is made of, together with its loft, the type of shaft, which is extremely important, and the grips you should have fitted.

The club head

Materials There are five main materials now in use:

● **Persimmon** This starts life as a solid block of wood from which only a very few skilled clubmakers create, by hand, wonderful golf clubs, beautifully finished in stains and lacquers and still sought after by some top professionals.

● **Wood laminate** Very few of these clubs are being produced now due to the metal takeover. These clubs were very popular in the recent past as they were much less expensive than persimmon. They are made from strips of wood glued together into blocks under pressure and then turned into golf clubs on a lathe.

Above and top: Traditional persimmon heads. Right and far right: Wood laminate heads made from wooden strips.

Equipment

● **Steel** Most of the top end of the market now belongs to steel. These clubs are cast in mouldings much like their iron counterparts. This gives very high control over the head shape and consistency of manufacture. Steel accounts for a large proportion of the clubs sold today.

● **Alloy** Pitched at the lower end of the market, these clubs are produced in much the same way as steel clubs, but the raw material costs help to keep the price down.

● **Carbon** Very much at the expensive end of the market, carbon is one of the hardest materials available and is used to produce some very fine clubs. However, the price is prohibitive for most people.

● **Others** There are other materials used to manufacture the heads of golf clubs, kevlar, the material used in bullet-proof vests, being just one that has been experimented with in recent times. The experiments will continue no doubt, but

none of these other materials has a significant place in the market at the moment.

How does the material the club is made from affect your game? The answer is in what the material allows the manufacturer to do with the construction of the golf club.

Wood, being the same density throughout, means that a club made from it will have a very definite centre of gravity. This centre will be quite small and, as only a centred strike will

Above and above right: Metal heads have an enlarged sweet spot.

12

Left and above: Carbon heads, the best in modern golf club technology but very expensive for most golfers.

produce the best results, the club made from wood is quite demanding of the player's ability.

Although metal is still very dense, it has properties that allow the manufacturer much more scope. The fact that it can be worked with while molten is the biggest factor in the production of metal drivers. This enables the club to be made quite differently to its wooden counterpart. It now does not have to be the same density all the way through; in fact the metal head is a fairly thin shell of metal with a much less dense material inside. This has the effect of concentrating the main weight of the club around its perimeter, enlarging the area of the club face from which you will achieve an effective shot. In golf we call this effective area of the face the club's 'sweet spot' and the key fact is that a metal driver's sweet spot is larger than that of a wooden one. This makes it more forgiving to an off-centred strike which is a great boon to all and is the reason I recommend metal drivers.

Equipment

Head size

This is a very topical subject. The large-headed tennis racquet has been with us for some time, and now the large-headed golf club has arrived. This continues the principle of enlarging the effective centre of the club, the sweet spot. If the club is bigger, the sweet spot is bigger! But is big beautiful?

Well, this is not entirely true; you still have to swing the club, and at a reasonable speed if you are going to hit the ball any distance. There is clearly a trade-off here. I can only draw a parallel again with tennis. Having flirted with the big heads, most tennis players have come back to mid-size. However, the head is certainly bigger than it was, and you do not see many wooden-framed racquets at Wimbledon these days.

The concept of the big-headed driver is still quite new and conse-

The photo shows from left to right: large, mid-size and normal head sizes.

quently the clubs themselves are still quite expensive. Try the trial clubs: if you love them, have them, but if not, I do not think that you will be held back by opting for a normal-sized metal head.

Club face loft

This is another emotive subject, as everyone tends to think that the less lofted the club the further you will hit the ball. Wrong! The club's loft must suit the power of the player using it. A strong striker will hit the ball further with a fairly straight-faced club, whereas a less powerful player will hit it further with a little extra loft. You must have the power available to get the ball properly airborne to achieve your maximum distance.

Think of those great, strapping athletes, the shot putters, javelin and discus throwers. None of them attempt to project their objects parallel to the ground. They are launching them upwards as well as forwards to achieve the maximum distance. Not too high, not too low – this is the same principle as your drive.

But what about the roll, I hear you ask? Well this is indeed a factor. It will change from lush, green fairways in spring to a hard-baked summer brown. The fact is that roll is too much of a variable to become a consideration in club choice.

Loft is also a factor in how accurate your shots will be. The straighter the face of the club, the more difficult it is to hit the ball consistently straight. This is due to:

1 The decrease in backspin a straight-faced club will put on the ball.
2 The increase in side spin produced by an open or closed club face at impact with a straight-faced club.

The table gives a good, general guideline to the loft suitable for players falling into the categories shown.

Desired loft based on modern metal drivers	
Children up to 12 years	15 degrees of loft
Children 12-14 years	13 degrees of loft
Boys 14-16 years	11 degrees of loft
Girls 14-16 years	12 degrees of loft
Men below 8 handicap*	8-10 degrees of lof
Women below 8 handicap*	10-11 degrees of loft
Men 8-20 handicap*	10-12 degrees of loft
Women 8-20 handicap*	11-12 degrees of loft
Men above 20 handicap	13-15 degrees of loft
Women above 20 handicap	13-15 degrees of loft
*Add one degree if aged over 50 and two degrees if over 60.	

Equipment

Club shaft

The science of the golf club shaft is extremely complex. It truly is a science, with large budgets committed to laboratory research and development in an attempt to continually improve the shaft and what it can do for the player. Design and technology have come a long way since hickory, and some knowledge of that progress will help you to understand better where we are today. Ultimately this will help you to choose the correct shaft for your game.

The main function of the shaft is to help to generate power. As it flexes and then works to regain its original shape, it increases the speed at which the club head is travelling, and therefore increases the distance the player is able to hit the ball. Clearly, if you were to play with a solid steel shaft, it would not flex at all during the swing, the result being a very short shot indeed. This idea of a solid steel shaft also introduces the element of weight; a solid shaft would be much heavier making it very difficult for you to move the club reasonably quickly, again reducing the distance attainable.

However, power is not the only factor in a good golf shot; accuracy is of equal value. Here again, the shaft has an important role to play. The shaft must be consistent and predictable in the way that it reacts to the swinging movement so that this accuracy is possible.

To sum up, a golf shaft has to be light enough to be able to swing easily – the lighter the better. It must be strong enough to react consistently to the stresses of the golf swing, providing accuracy, and it must be flexible, helping the player to generate increased club head speed and extra distance, which is often a tall order.

The early clubmakers started, as you probably know, with hickory. Hickory was flexible and strong enough to give consistency in its movement. However, it did not last for ever, and after continued use the shaft became tired, losing its ability to recover its shape quickly and therefore becoming less efficient. It had other problems: being solid it was quite heavy, and due to the fibrous nature of wood, it was susceptible to 'torque'. Torque is the condition that refers to the ability of a golf club shaft to rotate around its longitudinal axis. This causes a situation during the swing where the club face is no longer in its original relationship to the grip of the club or the player's hands, but displaced due to the twisting effect, or torque, of the shaft. Thus torque can have a serious effect on the direction of the shot.

Tubular steel was a major breakthrough. It was lighter than hickory, stronger than hickory, and did not suffer the material fatigue. It flexed well and all but eliminated the torque problems, and although the purists said it did not feel as good as hickory, steel was here to stay!

As you know, tubular steel is still the most popular shaft on the market today. It has not stood still over the years since its birth. Through modern technology, it has become lighter and lighter while still retaining its strength and flexibility.

Steel has seen a few challengers to its supremacy, however. Aluminium came, worked well in the short term, but did not have the strength to stand up to the rigours of golf. Many shafts broke after a relatively short time and the market soon lost confidence in it as a contender.

Carbon mounted its original challenge more than 10 years ago. It was very light, it had the strength and flexibility, but it reintroduced torque, and many players just could not keep their shots sufficiently straight with it. Some players, mainly women tour professionals, used the shaft with great results, and have played with it ever since. This gave carbon a slice of the market and established the idea of playing with this shaft in people's minds. The research continued, culminating in the release of the new generation of carbon shafts some five years ago. Torque was now totally under control, indeed the shaft could be made with any amount of torque from less than steel to slightly more. The only drawback is that carbon shafts are expensive, which is prohibitive to many golfers.

Carbon mounted its original challenge more than 15 years ago. It was steel still has the lion's share.

Let us go on to look at just what is available, and make sure that you are in the best position to decide what is best for your game.

Material

Steel: still the largest proportion of the market.

Carbon: increased greatly in popularity in recent years.

Carbon with boron tip: reserved for strong hitters.

Others: very small proportion of the market.

The biggest difference dictated by the material is in the weight of the shaft. This indeed was the biggest advantage of tubular steel over hickory. As long as the shaft remains strong and flexible, any weight that can be saved is a big bonus. It means that the club manufacturers can reduce the overall weight of the club while still retaining its normal playing characteristics, thereby making it more manageable during the swing.

Material	Players best suited
Steel	Good all-round shaft for all players
Carbon	Best for the less strong player
Carbon with boron tip (gold shaft)	Strong players only

Torque

Torque describes the shaft's tendency to rotate around its longitudinal axis during the swing. This tendency is to be found in all golf shafts to a greater or

Equipment

lesser degree. It has come to the fore in recent years due to the increased use of carbon-based shafts, and is only worth consideration for this type of shaft. In the table, I have used steel as the yardstick to grade the others against.

Again, the key is to match the torque with the strength of the player in order to maximize distance while retaining the accuracy of shot.

Degree of torque		Players best suited
Low torque:	less than steel	Very strong players
Mid torque:	the same as steel	Male mid-handicap players
Higher torque:	slightly more than steel	Weaker male and lady players

Below: This photograph shows the shaft flexing at the moment of impact to help the player achieve better club head speed and distance.

Driving

Shaft flex

The shaft flexes during the golf swing in order to help the player achieve club head speed and therefore distance. It is true to say that the more flexible the shaft, the more potential there is for increasing the distance the ball will fly. However, there is a down side to this equation: it also means there is an increased chance of an inaccurate strike and a poorly directed shot.

Most players will do best with a fairly standard shaft flex – men's regular for men, and women's regular for women.

Shaft flex	Players best suited
X: Extra stiff	Only very strong professional players
S: Stiff	Most professionals and young, low-handicap amateur men
R: Regular	The majority of male players
A: Amateur	Weaker men and stronger women
L: Ladies	The majority of female players

If you feel in need of some distance, and you are generally an accurate player, try a club fitted with the shaft below the group you feel best describes your golf in the shaft flex table.

If you are a powerful player in need of some directional help, opt for a club fitted with the shaft above the group that you feel best describes your golf.

Kick point

This is just a technical name for the way a golf club shaft flexes rather than the flex itself. The shaft can be constructed to flex nearer to the head of the club (low kick point), in the middle of the shaft (mid kick point), or nearer the grip end (high kick point). Each of these is suited to a certain type of player. Again, follow the table as a good, general guide.

Kick Point	Best suited players
High kick point	Strong male player looking for help to keep the ball down
Mid kick point	Standard shaft for most club players
Low kick point	High handicap or elderly players who experience difficulty in getting the ball airborne

All of these shafts are available in men's and ladies' flexes.

Length

The standard length for a driver is 43 inches for men, and 42 inches for women. Adding length to the shaft is certainly a way of increasing club head speed and therefore the distance of shot. This is a very popular ploy with club manufacturers today: most companies have a long driver in their catalogues. It is best to remember that extra shaft length also demands extra control. Unless you are particularly in need of added yardage on your drive, and are, on the whole, a very accurate player, standard length is probably best.

Equipment

Grips

Many players are very neglectful of the golf club grip. You may take your time choosing a club and look at all the areas already discussed, but if you play with the incorrect grip size for your hands, you will undo much of that good work. Your only connection to the club is through your hands via the grip. What could be more important than that?

It has to be said that the vast majority of players will be best suited to a standard size grip, the regular fitting for both ladies and men. However, it is important to make sure that this is right for you – a grip that is too thick for the player using it will often produce a slice; too thin, the converse, a hook.

In choosing the correct grip thickness, you need to be able to take hold of the various sizes of grip. This cannot be done until the grip has been fitted to a shaft. It will be of no use at all to test for grip thickness on unfitted grips. Take up your normal grip and make sure that you can get your hands comfortably around the grip. Check to see if your fingers are sticking into the flesh of your hands: if this is the case, the grip is too thin for you. If you cannot comfortably take up your normal grip and your hands feel under some pressure to hold on, then the grip is too thick. This is a very crude test but all in all probably the best way of choosing the correct grip thickness for your hand size.

Above right: The hold position which is achieved when the grip is the correct thickness for the player Right: Too thin a grip causes the left hand to be in a poor position.

Driving

Equipment

Equipment selection

As you will now realise, with all these aspects to consider, club selection is quite a difficult business. You will need some sound advice if you are a relatively inexperienced golfer, and for this help I would recommend that you contact a qualified PGA Professional. He (or she) has a wealth of experience which will be invaluable in helping you make the

correct choice of club. Often he will have trial clubs enabling you to hit some balls with several clubs before you part with your hard-earned cash.

Do not be put off by the technical language. Decide how much money you are prepared to spend on your new club. Spend up to the upper limit you have set yourself. There are very few bargains around, and you get what you pay for. If it is less expensive, the club will not be as well balanced or made to as strict a specification during the manufacturing process. Above all, do not make any snap decisions. Try the club out if a trial club is available, be certain about your choice, and you will be confident with the club. Rush in, make an impulse purchase, and the first few poor shots (an inevitability with any club) may just rock you enough to lose that all important confidence.

I would always commend you to a metal headed, standard shaft length club. The shaft material choice will depend largely on how much you wish to spend. The loft, shaft flex and kick point should be compatible with your standard of play, and the tables earlier in this section should give you a good idea of what you require. With the information in this section and some advice from a qualified professional, I feel sure that you will make a good choice.

Left: The range of modern shafts shows from left to right: flex twist carbon, boron tipped carbon (the gold shaft), a normal carbon shaft, and lightweight steel.

Caring for your equipment

It is really a very simple task to make sure that you take care of your equipment as long as you do it on a regular basis.

Golf club heads

Wooden
1 Always use headcovers.
2 Never leave headcovers on your clubs when they are wet.
3 Clean with a damp cloth.
4 If the lacquer becomes chipped or worn allowing water to penetrate through to the wood, have the club refinished by a qualified professional.

Metal
1 Always use headcovers.
2 Clean with soapy water and a soft brush.

Carbon
1 Always use headcovers.
2 Clean with a damp cloth.
3 Polish with a little furniture polish and a soft cloth.

Golf club shafts

- **Steel** This requires very little maintenance.
- **Carbon** A long-necked headcover is essential to protect the shaft.

Golf club grips

1 Keep them clean with warm soapy water and a nail brush.
2 If your grips become hard and shiny, get them renewed!

Now that you have your club, make sure that you look after it!

Headcovers will help protect your clubs, whether they are of wood or metal construction. Use during the round and also when transporting them in the car.

CHAPTER TWO

The grip

Tony Moore

Holding the golf club correctly ('the grip') is most important as its relationship with the club face dictates the type of swing and the shape of the shot the golfer will make. Selecting the most appropriate grip to suit your age, strength and swing together with taking care and attention every time you hold the club are essential if you wish to play consistent golf irrespective of whether you are young, old, and of high or low handicap. Placing the hands incorrectly on the golf club is a common reason for playing bad shots. In this chapter we will discuss grip selection and describe how to hold the club properly in order to achieve greater consistency when making shots.

The grip

Ways to grip a golf club

There are three commonly used grips, often selected arbitrarily by the golfer – the overlap or Vardon grip, the interlocking grip and the baseball grip. It is important that both hands work together when making a shot and this aim is best achieved if the palms of each hand are parallel when you hold the club. Therefore you should select the grip that suits you best if you are to achieve this aim. In order to do this, let us consider each in turn. We will explain how to form each grip later in this chapter.

Overlap grip
The overlap grip is the most popular way to hold the golf club. It was originated

by Harry Vardon who was alleged to have large hands, like bunches of bananas! Golfers with large or average sized hands (i.e. if you take a medium, large or extra large size in golf glove) are recommended to use this method. The pictures below show different versions of this grip. You will see that, for the right-handed golfer, the little finger of the right hand is placed either on top of the index finger of the left hand or in the gap between the index finger and second finger. Another form of this grip, which is commonly used by some golfers to grip the putter and to play pitch and run shots, is the reverse overlap where the index finger of the left hand is placed over the little finger

of the right hand. This grip tends to alter wrist action and should not be used in general play. The conventional overlap grip is the one most commonly used at all levels of golf.

Interlocking grip

The second method, the interlocking grip, is shown below. This time the little finger of the right hand and the index finger of the left hand interlock – hence the grip's name. This method of holding the club is often the most comfortable one and the best for golfers with short fingers as it links the hands together for those who find it difficult to set the little finger over the index finger. The great Jack Nicklaus, who indeed has short fingers, used the interlocking grip to excellent effect.

Baseball grip

The third grip is the baseball grip, which is sometimes called the full-finger or 'two-handed' grip, in which all eight fingers are placed on the handle of the club. The hands are placed in such a way that the little finger of the right hand and the index finger of the left hand touch each other without overlapping.

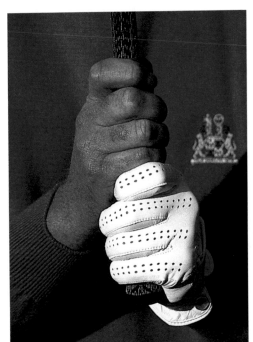

This photo shows that the back of the hands should be parallel to the club face.

Beginners often start with this grip, usually as a result of not having lessons with a professional but also because it is perhaps the easiest and most natural

Key tip

Whatever grip you choose always make sure that the palms of each hand are parallel to ensure that maximum consistency is achieved.

The grip

way to grip a golf club. Although this grip offers the greatest control of the club head, for golfers who wish to progress to low handicaps and those who wish to achieve maximum distance the baseball grip will be disadvantageous. If you hold the club using this method, it is important to ensure that the hands are as close together as possible and work in unison. Because the hands are not linked, the baseball grip may give rise to more inconsistency regarding the position of the hands on the handle of the club, and therefore care must be taken to ensure that the palms of the hands are always parallel.

Which grip should you choose?

The grip you choose will vary according to your age, strength and the size of your hands. Let us first of all consider age. If you are a young junior golfer the baseball grip is probably the most suitable for you, particularly if you have small fingers. Using this grip will allow you to generate greater grip strength which will help you to control the path of the club and club face in the swing. As your hands get larger and as you become stronger you should try to use the overlap grip or the interlocking grip. These will enable you to develop better control of the swing and ensure that your hands are working together to produce the best and most powerful shot. We have already said that the interlocking grip may be better for those golfers with short fingers.

The senior golfer will find that grip strength and feel will decrease with age; conditions such as arthritis, more frequent injuries and general wear and tear of the joints complicate matters when trying to grip the club. Pain when holding the club often causes the older golfer to develop an undesirable shuffle to the most comfortable position. In addition the senior golfer tends to hit the ball with less body action and more with the hands and arms. Adaptation to the situation is often required by grip modification.

Women may use any of the three grips described depending on the size of their hands and the length of their fingers. Women with small hands, however, may find it very difficult to use the overlap method and those who fall into this category should try to use the baseball grip.

Why you should have a good grip

The grip controls the way in which your hands help generate club head speed in your swing which, in turn, affects the distance you hit the ball. In addition, the grip greatly influences the swing path of the club head and determines whether or not the club face will be square at ball impact, making it fly straight or otherwise. The ball will slice or hook due to an open or closed club face at impact. The grip is not the only reason for erratic shots and you should also consider the other important parts of the swing described later in this book. Building a good grip, however, will make the task of hitting the golf ball much easier with more consistent results. For most players, consistency is the name of the game: if you could guarantee hitting the ball straight every time, you could knock shots off your handicap.

Tips for the older golfer

Fossils, Old Boys, call us what you will.... it seems such a shame that after many years of golf our bodies become weak, lose their suppleness and flexibility and our poor old joints seize up with arthritis. Although we can now think a great game, our ailments do not allow us to play as well as we used to. Wrists and fingers are among the first joints to be affected as we age and this may condition the way in which the golf club can be gripped. Some compensation is therefore required. Although it is not recommended that the type of grip is changed, using a slightly weaker grip may be advantageous but how ever the grip is modified, it is still essential that the palms of the hands remain parallel.

The grip

How to form your grip

Many golfers take a club out of the bag and take up the grip by shuffling the hands around until a comfortable position is reached, only to find the shot produced goes off in a different direction to the one intended, often in a fearsome arc which is honed in to the deepest rough or another hazard. In order to avoid this, you need to establish a set routine when gripping the club, based on the following principles.

Hold the club out in front of you with the right hand so that the toe of the club head is pointing skywards. This, rather than gripping the club when pointing downwards, will help to ensure that the forearms adopt a natural position at address. Open the left hand

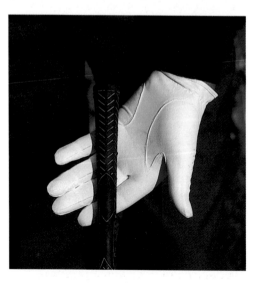

and place the handle of the club on the middle joint of the index finger. Wrap the finger around the handle and then angle the handle across the palm, beneath the fleshy part of the pad of the

hand (below left). Close the fingers around the handle. The hand should be placed so that about half an inch of the club grip shows above the back of the hand (some grips have a line around the top of the grip – this is a good guide line). The thumb is placed on the handle so

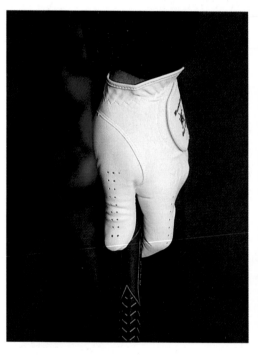

that it extends approximately one inch further down the shaft than the index finger, and the hand is rotated around the handle until, when the club is still outstretched in front of you, two to three knuckles of the left hand can be seen clearly in the photo above.

Place the right hand on the lower part of the handle closing it so that the base of the fingers grip the club. There should be a slight gap between the index finger and the middle finger. Adjust the

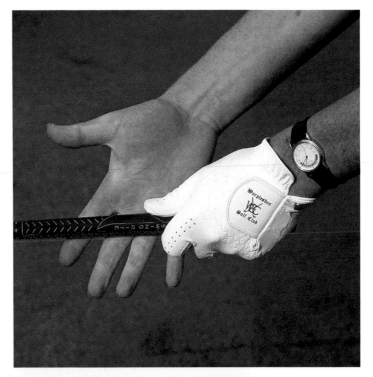

hand so that the palm of the right hand is parallel with the cutting edge of the club head as shown in the photo above.

If you are to use the **overlap grip** the right hand then slides up the handle so that the little finger overlaps the index finger of the left hand and the fleshy part of the palm at the base of the right thumb covers the whole of the left thumb. The index finger and thumb of the right hand should then touch.

If you have decided to use an **interlocking grip**, the left hand placement is the same but this time the little finger of the right hand interlocks with the index finger of the left hand completing a grip similar to the one shown on page 27.

Identical principles are used if you choose a **baseball grip.** This time the right hand slides up the handle until the

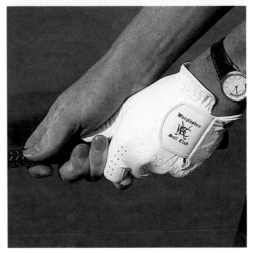

Above and left: These two photos show the overlap grip with the right hand open (above) and the little finger already in position, and the fingers closed around the grip (left).

hands touch, but the fingers do not overlap or interlock and all eight fingers hold the club. The thumb of the left hand is still covered by the fleshy part of the palm at the base of the right thumb.

It is better to slide the right hand up to the left hand to ensure that both

The grip

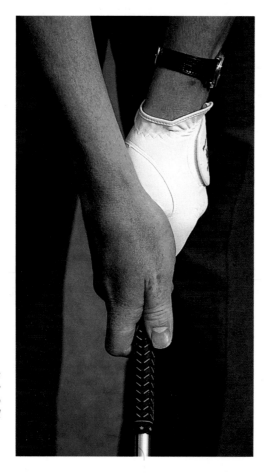

Right: This shows the overlapping grip in its final position.

hands take up the correct position. Assembling the grip with both hands at the same time can promote shuffling both hands into incorrect positions.

You should study the pictures in this chapter and try each grip to find the one you feel most comfortable using. If you are already hitting the ball well with one of these grips, don't change; simply try to improve your current method using the procedures described above.

Grip tightness

You should not grip the club so tightly that your fingers go white – this will tend to cause tension and reduce natural wrist action which in turn will give rise to a loss of distance in your shots. If you grip the club too loosely, however, you may allow the club face to turn on impact or you may even see the club following the ball after hitting it! Imagine that you are holding an open tube of toothpaste – if you grip too tightly the toothpaste will come out. You should hold the tube as tightly as you can without this happening, and this is the ideal grip tightness. Sometimes during a round your swing gets faster, you grip the club more tightly and you try to hit the ball hard for maximum distance. Try to relax when you address the ball and start by letting your hands relax on the grip – this, in turn, will enable the muscles in your forearm to relax. Muscle tension may be created by having too tight a grip which in turn leads to a reduction in flexibility and suppleness during the swing.

For those who use the overlap or interlocking grips, you should find that the little and third fingers of the right hand and the middle two fingers of the left hand contribute most when holding the golf club.

Weak grips and strong grips

You have probably heard these expressions but you may have no idea what they mean. It is really quite simple. If your grip is too strong, the position of the hands are too far to the right, i.e. under the handle, and this will cause the club face to be closed at impact leading you to hook the ball. An example of what a strong grip looks like can be seen in the photograph. An opposite fault is to have a weak grip in which the hands are placed too far to the left (i.e. over the handle) which causes the ball to slice. In this case the hands need to be adjusted so that a more neutral grip is achieved.

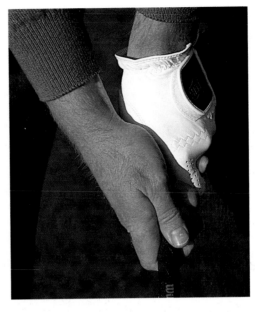

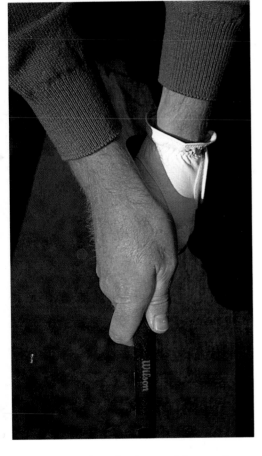

Far left: A weak grip with the hands positioned too far to the left. Left: A strong grip with the hands too far to the right.

them both to generate greater leverage through the shot and also to hit more powerfully.

Altering the grip to draw and fade the ball

Your standard grip should be used to hit shots with any club. In some cases, the more experienced or low-handicap golfer may wish to generate deliberate hooks (draws) or slices (fades). This may be done by modification of the grip and stance. A draw is the result of adjusting the hands to a strong position and aligning the body so that the stance is closed. Alternatively, a fade may be generated by taking up a weak grip and aligning the body so as to adopt an open stance. Trying to draw and fade the ball is difficult and the average golfer need only ever try to hit the ball straight! It is often good fun, however, to experiment on the practice range but preferably not on the golf course in a club competition.

Often people playing with weak or strong grips hit the ball straight – this is usually due to another fault in the swing which corrects the grip problem. The golf swing is controlled by many factors and solving a grip problem may only be the start of you rebuilding your swing.

Women often find it advantageous to use a slightly strong grip. This helps

The grip

Right: The correct way to put on a glove. Do not pull the glove on, but ease your fingers in gently pushing the material into the gaps between them.

How to check your grip

The simplest way to check your grip is to follow a set routine, as described. Even the most experienced golfer will not always grip the club in exactly the same way each time. The more you play, you will find that before each shot your grip will vary slightly. A common cause of 'losing form' is when your grip becomes lazy and you take up a position that gets slightly worse after each shot.

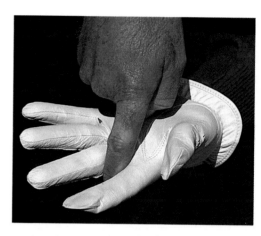

Key tip

Check your grip frequently – memorize what a good grip looks like. If you are having troubles on the course make sure that your grip is not the cause.

Unconventional grips

Some golfers use a reverse grip, whereby for the right-hander the right hand is positioned at the top of the club and the left hand is placed below the right hand. Although this may lead to striking the ball reasonably well, it is not recommended and will lead to a reduction in the distance the ball is hit.

Ways to assist gripping the club

Many players choose to wear a golf glove. There are now many types of material used in their construction but the most common dry weather glove is made of soft leather. The glove should fit the hand snugly so that there is no slack. A new glove should feel slightly tight until the leather stretches. This is especially important as the fit of the glove may greatly affect your ability to grip the golf club and it is important to seek advice when buying your first glove. In wet weather, leather gets very slippery and you should put away this type of glove in favour of an 'all weather' glove made from synthetic materials. You will also find rubber gloves on sale; the aim of all weather and rubber gloves is to increase your ability to hold the club appropriately in adverse conditions without having to squeeze the club tightly, thereby introducing tension in the hands, wrists and forearms.

The way a golf glove wears is a good guide to how well you grip and swing the club. If your glove gets holes in the palm or thumb soon after you have bought it, the reason is unlikely to be the poor quality of the glove. Indeed, it is more likely to be a sign that your grip and swing need some modification.

Another way to assist your play is to select the correct thickness of grip on your club. If your grips are too thick, this will lead to a reduction in wrist and hand action causing slower club head

Exercises to assist grip strength

Fitness is an important part of any sport. You may improve your ability to grip the golf club by strengthening the small muscles in your hands and wrists. The following exercises may help:

● Twist a towel one way and then the other.
● Place a squash ball in the palm of the hand and repetitively squeeze it.
● Instead of normal press-ups, try fingertip press-ups.

speed and hence loss of distance, together with a slice. Having too thin a grip, particularly if you have big hands, will not help when trying to adopt the correct hand positions. Again, the advice of your local professional may be useful in determining your ideal grip thickness. Some golf club manufacturers take grip thickness into consideration when customizing a set of golf clubs.

There are three main types of golf club grip – normal, half cords and full cords. Modern production methods allow rubber grips to be interwoven with cord. The use of this in the whole club grip (full cord) or in half the club grip allows the golfer to retain better contact with the club, thereby minimizing club slip in wet weather or when the hands are sweating on hot summer days (or when nervous!). For the lady golfer, however, cord grips often cause soreness or hard areas of skin on the hands, and

normal soft grips are recommended. Old golf clubs may be fitted with leather grips, which may well be splitting at the joins. If the grip on the club is worn or damaged, this will not help the golfer achieve the maximum benefit when holding the club.

Now try it....!

In this chapter we have addressed some of the important points regarding holding the golf club. If you are just starting the game, I hope that the tips given here will help you formulate the most suitable grip and also to hold the club correctly. Remember that the grip will not only determine the direction in which the ball will travel but it will also influence how far the ball will go after you have hit it. If the hands and wrists work together, which can be achieved only by using a proper grip, you will become a more consistent golfer and at least be able to hit the ball straight almost every time. For the more experienced golfer, always try to improve your grip by checking your hand positions frequently and ensure that your palms are parallel. Try also to develop a set routine to ensure that hand position will be the same every time and thus minimize the chances of losing form because of taking up a careless grip.

Key tip

A good grip leads to a healthy swing; your hands are a key way to communicate with the club head and control the club face.

CHAPTER THREE

The set up

Alisdair Barr

As golf is played with a stationary ball, your preparation to make the swing is extremely important. The swinging movements are determined by the manner in which you stand or 'set up' to the ball. The golfing muscles can be positioned so that they can fulfil the movements that you want them to make. The tournament Professional is at great pains to get this position correct so it is vital that we follow his lead. We may not be able to swing as well as perhaps Nick Faldo or Seve Ballesteros, but there is no reason why we cannot achieve their good set up and at least give ourselves a reasonable chance of producing a successful stroke. When all is said and done, the top pros only have two hands, two legs and two feet like us, so let's try and copy what the best golfers do. It is also true to say that most swing faults stem from a suspect start, so it is vital to get it right.

The set up

Elements of the set up

Now let's look at the stages that go into this important position. It is also important that the sequence is adhered to so that nothing is missed out. The set up sequence is as follows:

1 **Aim** The blade of the club head.
2 **The hold** (or grip) of the club.
3 **Posture** The position of the spine and legs (your poise).

4 **Stance** The actual position of the feet.
5 **Body alignment** Aiming your body, feet, hips and shoulders, in the direction you want the ball to travel.
6 **Ball position** Relative to the player's feet.

Let's now look at each element in detail.

Aim

Below: With two clubs on the ground, one representing the ball-to-target line and the other the ball position, you can see how the leading edge of the club face is at 90 degrees to the ball-to-target line.

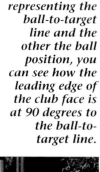

Right: The overall set-up position showing the club head in the aimed or square position.

It may seem very obvious that the club should be pointed in the correct direction, but it is important that you understand how to do it.

First of all, you have to imagine a line drawn on the grass from the ball to the target – we refer to this as the target line. Everything that you do with regard to the target and aiming is referred to this line.

To position the club we refer to the leading edge which is the bottom front edge of the club head. This leading edge is positioned at right angles to the target line with the sole or bottom of the club resting on the ground. This club face position is referred to as being 'square': the club is lying correctly for itself and aimed in the proper direction. It is important that you check the blade regularly throughout the set-up routine as the slightest change can affect the overall result greatly.

The grip

The grip, or hold, has already been dealt with in a previous chapter but do remember to assemble the grip with the club head already in the aimed position. I find that a lot of beginners will twist the club out of position while assembling the grip and are then reluctant to take their hands off the club to put it back in position. This is understandable but does not encourage consistency. The photo sequence below and overleaf shows my preferred teaching method.

Left: This illustrates the left hand and arm hanging naturally by your side.

The set up

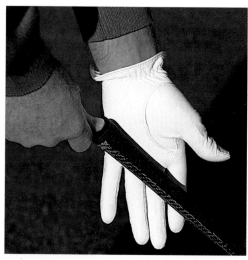

Left: The left hand is introduced to the grip of the club at this angle (with the fingers pointing to the ground and not with the hand held bent at the wrist). Above: This illustrates perfectly the angle at which the grip passes through the hand.

Below: The 'V' shape formed between the thumb and forefinger will point between the chin and right shoulder. This position is flexible, due to the size of the hand.

Above and right: The hand is closed round the handle with the left thumb just right of centre and two to three knuckles visible on the back of the hand.

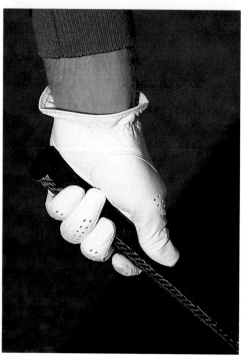

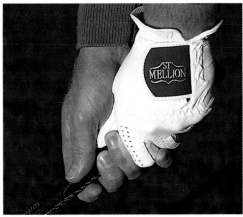

Left: The right hand is introduced again with the fingers pointing at the ground. This shows the angle. The little finger is already in the overlapped position.
Above: The right hand has been closed round the handle with the palm pointing at the target, in line with the back of the left hand.

Posture

Without good posture it is impossible to have good balance throughout the swing, and if there is loss of balance there will be total loss of control. Good balance comes from the poise of the player. Your posture will control the angle of attack of the club head on the downswing and will therefore determine the quality of the strike. Correct posture can only be achieved in one way, and it is determined by the height of the player and the club being used.

Stand as tall as you can using your full height, with your arms hanging freely in front of you. Bend forwards from the hips (or over the buckle of your belt) until the club head touches the grass. The amount of bend will vary from club to club depending on the

length of the shaft. This will bring the weight automatically forwards on to the balls of the feet. The spinal angle will remain in its natural position and this will allow the head position to stay constant throughout the swing.

As one part of the body goes forwards, another automatically goes back so at this point you will feel your knees tightening. To ease the pressure, soften or bend the knees slightly. This will relax your body and encourage a smooth swing.

Your head should be held clear of the chest and this will give the feeling of holding the body 'up'. It should also be turned slightly to the right. This will encourage a full body turn in the backswing as it creates space for the left

The set up

shoulder to work. Do not overdo this position as it will cause the left shoulder to drop at the start of the backswing and also cause loss of height.

If this position is achieved in reverse and your legs are positioned first, it creates a feeling of 'sitting down' and your body weight will be back on the heels. The old adage of sitting down on a coffee stool or shooting stick has long been discarded. Anything athletic has to be performed from the front end of the shoes and not the back. The head must not be kept down, another golfing myth, as this will cause overall restrictions on the backswing and a very cramped follow through.

This sequence demonstrates the way to assume correct posture. Above: Stand at full height with the arms extended so that the club shaft is parallel to the ground. Top right: Bend from the hips until the club head touches the ground (the amount of bend is controlled by the length of the club shaft). The legs straighten as a direct result of this. Right: Soften the knees to remove pressure from the legs and spine.

Stance

The widest part of anyone's body is across the shoulders, and therefore a base is needed to support them. Your feet form that base and must be positioned approximately shoulder width apart. As the shaft of the club becomes

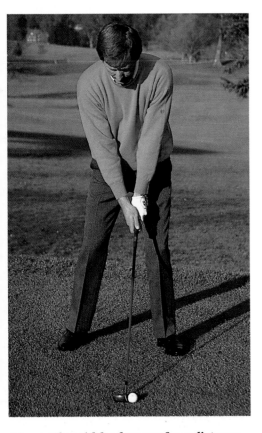

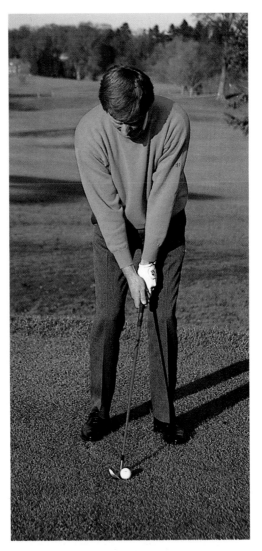

Above: The width of stance for a distance club is approximately the width of the shoulders and the weight evenly distributed. Above right: As the club shaft shortens, the stance can narrow (the club being used here is a wedge).

shorter so the stance can be slightly narrowed. The shorter swing is not so full and therefore not so physical, and a narrow stance will suffice. The feet are

placed basically as you would walk, although a guide line here is to have the left foot turned out slightly and the right one approximately half of the left. Again this is to encourage free movement throughout the swing. The body weight is distributed evenly, and the feeling should be that of being ready for physical activity.

43

The set up

Body alignment

As you have already aimed the blade to the target it is now time to position your body in the same direction. This is essential to avoid arguments between you, the player, and your club.

Your feet, hips and shoulders should be positioned parallel to the ball-to-target line we discussed when aiming the blade. The popular analogy is that of standing on a railway track with the club head on one rail and your feet on the other. To encourage good line up, you should adopt the following exercise.

Place the club behind the ball with the sole on the grass. Now take up your grip, still keeping the blade flat on the grass. The feet are now introduced but placed together. You can shuffle around until you feel a comfortable distance from the ball. When the feet are placed together the stance is so unsympathetic to the width of the shoulders that the

Above: The 'railway line'. The feet are positioned on one club shaft, and the club head on the other. With the shafts parallel, you are aimed correctly at the target. The feet do not point at the target; they will be slightly to the left but parallel to the ball-to-target line.

Above: The shoulders too will be parallel to the ball-to-target line. As the shoulders control the swing line it is vital to have them in this position.

44

body automatically stands in line with itself and the toes are always placed in line. A little imagination is needed here to visualize the line through the toes being parallel to the ball-to-target line. The feet are now separated with three things in mind:

1 The shoulder width stance.

2 The ball position, which, at this stage, we still have to discuss.

3 The line through the toes must remain the same.

When checking the alignment of the toes, hips and shoulders you will notice that they do not actually point at the target but to the left of it, although still parallel to the target line.

When practising at a later stage, it is advisable to position a club on the grass midway between the feet and ball and parallel to both, as this will give a good indication of the correct line-up and allow you to get the feel of it. Just as with the blade, we describe this as a 'square' stance.

This is a good exercise for you to practise to align the feet and achieve the correct ball position. Stand with the feet totally together and your feet, hips and shoulders will all be in line with themselves. Position the toes parallel to the ball-to-target line.

For the metal-headed club being used, take a small step with the left foot so that a line from the ball to the feet passes just inside the left heel. The step with the right foot is to complement that and make the feet shoulder width apart.

The set up

Ball position

Right: Although the ball position will change for the different clubs, the hand position is always just opposite the left thigh.

The hitting zone is from the middle of the stance forwards, and that is where you should position the ball. The longer the club, the further forward the ball should be positioned. For the wooden/metal headed clubs the line drawn from the ball to the feet should pass in line with the left heel. The ball will then be moved progressively back, approximately one inch per club. This will mean that by the time the 6 iron is reached the ball will be in the middle of the feet, and this is as far back as you need go for conventional shots.

During the swinging movement the club head is at its lowest point just left of centre. Prior to this the club head is on the downswing and immediately after it is on the up. If the ball is struck on the downswing the grooves on the club and the dimples on the ball combine to give the ball maximum backswing. This is desirable with the medium and shorter irons as you want the ball to stop the minute it hits the green. The last thing you want is for the ball to run on for ever as it would be very difficult to control the distance.

The bigger clubs require distance so you have to try and eliminate as much of the backspin as possible. To achieve this you need to strike the ball on the upswing, and that is the reason for the forward ball position.

There is a misguided belief that the wooden/metal headed clubs are hit with overspin to make the ball roll when it lands. This is not true as it would be

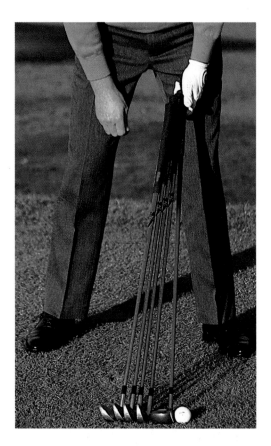

impossible to get the ball airborne.

Another school of thought on ball position suggests playing every club with the ball in line with your left heel and widening your right foot as the clubs get longer. The idea behind this system is that the fewer changes you make, the easier it is to be consistent. However, this forward ball position makes it more difficult to keep your shoulders in line with the target, particularly with the shorter clubs, i.e. the 8 and 9 irons.

Regardless of the system used, your hands are always opposite the inside of

46

your left leg. This will mean that even with a driver, your hands will be level with the ball. This is important because if your hands were behind the ball, a wristy or flicking action would follow. When the right passes the left hand all power has been used.

This completes the points that go into making a good set up, and you are now ready to build a golf swing. It is worth repeating at this stage that the good features in a golf swing are predetermined by the quality of your set up. A good player, who may be experiencing difficulty with his posture and overall set up, can in fact find the correct position by making a slow swing and freezing at the point he would consider to be the perfect impact position. By posing in this position he can then remove the momentum from his legs and place the club head behind the ball on the grass. If this is the position he knows he would like to adopt on impact, he can start off from here. After all, it must be easier to return to a position than to have to compromise and find another.

Above: You will notice that at the point of contact with the ball (or impact) the position of the body is the same as in the set up with regard to the arms, hands, club and head. The only difference is that momentum has carried the feet and legs forward towards the target.

Left: With the hands behind the ball, a high percentage of body weight is in front of the ball, and as soon as the right hand passes the left all the drive has been removed from the shot.

CHAPTER FOUR

The backswing

Alisdair Barr

Now that the set up has been completed successfully, your golfing muscles have been prepared to swing the golf club itself. The first part of the movement, the backswing, is again a means of preparation. You must position yourself and the ball in the correct direction and in a powerful fashion. Clearly, if you have completed the backswing correctly the forward swing has a distinct chance of being equally successful.

In this respect a good analogy is that of driving a motor car. No matter how well you drive it is impossible to go forward (should there be an obstacle in the way) without reversing. The car is therefore positioned in such a way that it is free to go forward at maximum speed. This describes the golf swing perfectly.

The backswing

Pre-swing routine

Just prior to swinging the club there are a couple of helpful movements which I wish to discuss: the waggle and the forward press.

The waggle

As you have prepared your body for physical movement, it can be quite a tense position. To help alleviate some of this tension a slight movement of the wrists taking the club back and forth on either side of the ball will help to ease this pressure.

To relax the feet and legs it is acceptable to move the weight slightly from foot to foot. This is all designed to help you from 'freezing' over the ball. I would strongly recommend that you adopt this movement in your swing routine.

Forward press

Again, to adopt the analogy of driving a car, the learner finds the most difficult thing is to have a smooth start to the swing procedure rather than a jerky start. How often do you see the 'kangaroo petrol' situation? So it is with the golf swing. A smooth takeaway will allow the swing to be in control. It does not have to be slow but it must be smooth or in tempo. To encourage this, a slight forward movement of the hands and wrists, while leaving the club head on the ground behind the ball will then create a recoil and so the backswing can be triggered in this way.

Rodger Davis, the fine Australian player who won the Professional Golfers Association Championship, is a firm believer in this particular movement. The 'forward press' can also be achieved, although not so commonly, by a slight 'kicking in' of the right knee, again creating the recoil discussed earlier. Gary Player from South Africa, whose record speaks for itself, has used this version of the 'forward press' for many many years. If you do find it difficult to get started in the backswing then I would suggest that you should experiment with both systems and select the one that you find most beneficial to your game.

The full set-up position. A very slight forward movement of the hands towards the target will help to create a slight recoil, thereby 'triggering' the backswing.

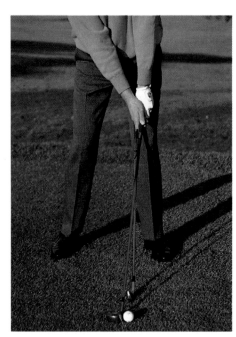

Building your swing

The successful golf shot requires two elements: direction and power. We now need to look in detail at the movements we have to make to encourage both of these things to happen in order to build a swing routine that will eventually lead to a consistent swing, the ingredient for which all golfers from Nick Faldo down have been searching.

To help build a swing it is advisable to start with a 6 or 7 iron. These clubs will make the ball travel far enough to let you see what you have achieved, but they are not power clubs, which are designed to send the ball a long way, so there is no undue pressure to hit the ball hard (or smash the living daylights out of the ball as a lot of learners feel the need to do!).

The takeaway

This is the first movement of the back-swing. It will encourage the directional side of the shot and will also encourage the club and your body to work together during the swing – an absolute must.

It is commonly referred to as the 'one piece' takeaway and it is just as valid now as when it was first suggested. The club is taken straight back from the ball for the first five to six inches. The club head will be on the target line and also parallel to the shoulders. The easiest way to achieve this is to keep the club head close to the ground. The feeling will be that the club head, shaft, left hand, arm and shoulder have all been moved together as one unit. The club is then allowed to continue to waist level and at this point you *stop*.

As a direct result of this one conscious movement, two very definite things will have happened:

1 Wherever the left arm goes the left shoulder must follow, so you will begin to see that shoulder appearing between your eyes and the ball. It is this turning of the shoulder that will start to take the club head inside or to the player's side of the ball-to-target line that we discussed in the previous chapter on the set up. At waist level there may be an impression that the club head is no longer on line and that it is facing away from the target. Some simple checks can be carried out to show that the club head and body have in fact stayed together.

- The leading edge of the club head will still be at right angles to the shoulders.
- The number of knuckles visible on the back of the left hand will be the same as in the set up.
- If a line was drawn from the feet to the ball, the club should have been taken back from this line at 90 degrees. If you now turn your whole body, feet included, and the club head is lowered back to the grass the relationship between club head and shoulders should be exactly the same as in the original set-up position.

The backswing

Above: The full set up from face on. Right: The set up looking down the target line. Far right: The one-piece takeaway (front on). So far it is really only a movement of the club head, the hands and arms. At this early stage you will not feel a great deal of movement from your shoulders and legs.

2 The second of the two responses to the takeaway is that the body weight will begin to transfer on to the inside edge of the right shoe. The left knee, as a direct result, will come towards the right knee and, depending on the club being used and therefore the ball position, will point to or just behind the ball. The right knee will remain flexed as in the set up. If you allow the right leg to straighten there will be a lifting action in the body and it would be extremely difficult to return to the impact position for the forward swing.

Neither the beginning of the shoulder turn nor the weight transference are positions with which you need concern yourself. They will happen automatically but it is as well that you are aware that this will happen and that you don't fight it. You are about to find out why!

Above: The same position looking down to the target.

Above: Halfway back. The wrists are now beginning to set or 'cock' (not a conscious movement), the left shoulder is becoming involved, and the club head starts to go slightly on the 'inside'. The body weight is now starting to transfer to the inside of the right foot. Top: The same position from behind but a clear indication of the club moving inside the line.

At waist level

At the waist level position we have what we refer to as a 'half swing' and the shoulders will have turned through approximately 45 degrees. This is about half of what they will turn so you can see that the club and body have stayed in 'synch'. If you were aligned correctly in the set up, and you find yourself in this position, then you should achieve good direction.

Key tip

If at waist level you discover that the shoulders have not turned enough, then the club head has been taken to the far side of the ball-to-target line. This usually happens because the club had been picked up or lifted by the wrists or a bending of the elbows.

On the other hand, if the shoulders have turned in advance of the hands, then the club head has been brought inside the line (the player's side) too quickly.

In either situation the club has not gone along the target line. A good exercise to encourage the correct line is to place a tee peg six inches behind the ball on the target line and train the club to hit it on the takeaway. If it is a line, even though it may not feel like it, then you will know that you must be correct.

The backswing

Swing check

The waist level check point: if the takeaway has been completed successfully the leading edge of the blade should be at right angles to the shoulders. This can be checked by turning the body 90 degrees to the right of a line drawn from the ball to the feet. If the club head is then placed back on the grass the relationship between the club head and shoulders should be the same as at the set up. This means that the club and body are working together.

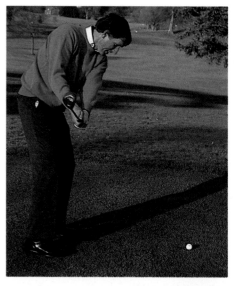

The second half of the backswing

This is where the power of the swing is taken into account. For the purposes of building a swing we break it down into two distinct movements; the second stage is really only a continuation of the first. Having invited the left shoulder into the swing we complete the backswing by continuing the turn until such time as the left shoulder is positioned between the chin and the ball. The shoulders will have turned through approximately 90 degrees, or as much as the suppleness of your body will allow.

Younger players clearly will find this a lot easier to do than the more mature person. It is this turn that dictates the length of the swing, not the height that the hands create. Just as at waist level, two things will have happened:

1 The weight will now have responded fully and it will be positioned over the right hip, knee and ankle.

2 There will be a feeling of torsion around the hips and the inside of the left leg. This is because the lower body has resisted the turn of the shoulders so that the hips will have rotated through only approximately 45 degrees. This

The shoulders and legs are really working at this stage. The left shoulder will be very visible as it starts to move under the chin and the left knee has moved inwards.

The backswing

Right: This photograph demonstrates quite clearly the response from the left leg to the 'one-piece' takeaway.

coiled, or 'wound up', feeling has been created, and it is the release of this tension that creates the hit. By being positioned on the right side, the left side has been prepared to accept the body weight as it drives forward. The left heel may well want to lift off the ground in the backswing and I suggest that you allow this to happen.

As you can see, the large muscles of the body – the shoulders and legs – have been fully employed, and this spring-like effect will be ready to 'explode' into action on the forward swing.

You will also notice that at the top of the backswing the wrists have hinged,

It is from approximately waist level that the movement is dictated by the left shoulder. You should now try to turn it sufficiently so that it is directly between the eyes and the ball. This will achieve the 90-degree turn you desire.

Above and right: The completed shoulder turn and weight transference. This will give you the 'wound up' feeling between the lower and upper body. This tension gives you something to release to initiate the power in the shot.

or 'cocked'. This happened automatically at around about waist level. It was caused by the weight of the head of the club and the momentum of the swing. Again, this is not something that you need concern yourself with, but do check that it has happened. The left arm will be *comfortably straight* (as you can see from the photographs) but by no stretch of the imagination could it be described as totally straight. What it must not do is to buckle under the pressure of the swing (if it has, it is your grip that needs attention).

The shaft of the club at the top of the backswing will be parallel to the ball-to-target line. It will actually be aiming slightly to the left but, as I have already said, related to the line. This

again means that the club is related to the target so it too is 'aimed', so to speak.

If the club aims to the left but is not parallel, it is said to be 'laid off'. However, if it is to the right of the target then it is across the line. Either of these faulty positions is caused by a suspect takeaway.

Summary

The speed of the golf swing is always controlled by how long it takes the large muscles to reach the top of the backswing so if you are aware of arriving at the top then you have performed the swing at a speed you can control. This allows you to find your own tempo. It does not matter if you have a quick, medium or slow tempo as, for example, Ian Woosnam, Seve Ballesteros or Nick Faldo have respectively. It is the swing that controls the rhythm. Slow is no guarantee of success but it would appear from a lot of my amateur friends that a slow tempo and keeping your head down are the keys to good golf!

Always remember that the bigger the wind up, the greater the release, and it should come as no surprise to learn that the really great players all have a good shoulder turn in common.

You are now fully prepared to strike the ball, so let's move on to the next part of the swing: impact.

CHAPTER FIVE

The impact zone

Nick Allen

Many golfers using a driver give the impression of making uncontrolled downswing movements that lead to hitting at the ball. Understanding the sequence of movement in the downswing and practising the following techniques will improve your ball flight pattern and general consistency. It is important to understand that the faults we observe in the downswing, while watching other golfers, are usually influenced by an earlier swing move or position. How the body has turned and its position at the top of the backswing are key factors and some of these positions influence the common downswing errors that we see.

The impact zone

Poor body turn

In the photographs the restricted body position at the top shows how the shoulders have not turned sufficiently, and the trunk is resisting the completion of the backswing, which forces the

Above and right: Because the shoulders have not completed a full turn, the body has restricted the hands and arms from completing the backswing. This resistance forces the hands to snatch the club, giving the impression of hitting at the ball.

hands and arms to start down prematurely by snatching the club. The correct weight transference cannot be achieved and the player appears to hit at the ball. A misconception frequently demonstrated is the player who drops the left shoulder at the start of the swing. At the top, the shoulder angle is too steep, a position that is known as 'tilted'; during the downswing, the club travels on a

steep arc forcing the player back (to the right) and restricting follow through.

During the takeaway lifting the left heel too much and swinging too far inside the line leads to an excessive hip turn; this forces weight on to the left side and encourages the shoulders to turn further than the required 90

Right: A swingpath that travels too far inside the line on the takeaway influences unrestricted hip turn. The shoulders turn beyond 90 degrees, the right side comes over the top and the weight moves on to the right side.

Driving

In the sequence above, the left shoulder drops sharply under the chin, caused by lifting the arms or sliding the hips. The angle of attack on the downswing is too steep, forcing the player backwards and restricting the follow through.

degrees. In the downswing the right side instinctively spins out, forcing weight on to the right leg.

All of the downswing symptoms mentioned here were influenced by poor body position at the top of the backswing. These errors promote a loss of power and force the player out of position during the downswing. There are many misconceptions regarding how the power source is created with the driver. A common one relates to the golfer with a muscular physique whose expectancy for distance is never realised; or the player who generates significant club head speed yet similarly does not drive the ball very far.

Above: Although tremendous swing speed has been generated, poor technique has limited the potential. The hands and arms are restricted by the body.

The impact zone

Timing

It is very important to understand the exact meaning of timing, which should be expressed as the correct sequence of movement in the swing; it does not relate to swing speed. Like an engine, if a single function within the cycle is not working, timing and full capacity are not reached. It naturally follows that in order to time the swing effectively your technique must be sound. Regardless of how strong the individual or how fast the club is swung, poor technique and

Above and right: The distance between the left shoulder and your hands at the top is the width of arc. A narrow width cannot provide power, but from a position of full width, you can achieve the maximum leverage and power.

timing will restrict your ability to drive the ball well. Observing the technique of tournament professionals will further enhance your understanding. Notice how some top players can generate extremely fast swing speed yet do not drive the ball any further (if at all) than a fellow competitor of lesser build.

At the top of the backswing there are three keys that allow you to deliver the driver correctly to the ball and realise your full potential for power. **Maximum width of arc** at the top refers to the distance between your left shoulder and hands; if you can achieve full width at the top you can generate greater leverage and power.

An imaginary line extending upwards and across your shoulders represents your **swing plane**; if your club merges with this line at the top, then it is in the perfect position to start the downswing.

These two positions are influenced by the **body turn** which is a primary factor at the start of the downswing. Spectators at a golf tournament are often surprised at how effortlessly top players drive the ball. This deception is linked to the function of the body in the swing. At the top of the backswing a correct turn produces a resistance between the upper and lower half of the body. The shoulders have turned approximately 90 degrees against a resistance from the hips, which turn through approximately 45 degrees. You should feel a stretching sensation which

Above and left: A line drawn from the club head across the shoulders represents your ideal swing plane. If the club merges with this line at the top, you are ideally positioned to start the downswing. Although your club may be slightly below the line, it should not be above it. These two positions are inter-related and influenced by body turn.

The impact zone

is your trunk continuing to turn as your hips resist. This is the major power position where the deception occurs when watching professionals.

The backswing and downswing merge together in response to the wound turn. As the backswing is completed and the body becomes fully wound, the lower body recoils in the same way. It is here that the deceptive nature of power becomes evident. The player is not attempting to produce

In this sequence, at the top of the backswing, the shoulders have turned through 90 degrees and the hips approximately 45 degrees. The backswing and downswing merge as the lower body muscles recoil in response to a good turn.

Left: The response of the hips recoiling influences the legs to drive laterally towards the target. This is another contribution to power. The hips are unwinding slightly earlier than the shoulders and the left hand is controlling the downward path by pulling the club.

Left: Many club golfers destroy the correct sequence of downswing movement by driving the legs and hips towards the target, blocking the passage of the hands and arms.

power by moving the hands and arms fast; the larger and stronger body muscles achieve this to repeat, not through conscious movement, a reaction recoil achieved from storing the power. The hips recoil and influence the legs to drive laterally towards the target – a further contribution to power.

The leverage (pull) of the left hand achieves two things: it maintains the correct plane and path of the downswing; and also it 'times' the recovery process as the wrists uncock. A strong leg drive in the downswing used to be prevalent with top players, many of

whom used what was called a reverse 'C' impact position. This was created by the force of the legs driving at the target, and forcing the trunk backwards.

Modern teaching prefers to control this movement within a more pivotal role of the body. However, many club golfers use the lower body in a way that destroys the timing of the downswing.

The impact zone

The legs and hips drive at the target and block the passage of the hands and arms through impact.

Similarly it is important to further understand the role of the left hand in the downswing. A common fault at the top of the backswing is to snatch with the hands. This encourages the body to straighten during the downswing and the wrists to uncock prematurely. Conversely, if the hands do not exert any influence on maintaining the path and plane in the downswing, the right side dominates and throws the club outside the line. The left hand pulls the

butt of the grip downwards with sufficient authority to control the path (not a snatch).

The length and lie of the club at address will promote the plane and angle of attack on the downswing. The shorter shaft and more upright lie with an iron allow the player to deliver the club from a steeper angle of attack (as

Above: The shorter length and more upright lie of an iron promote a steep angle of attack as the club head descends to impact.

opposed to a wood) where the club head is descending as it strikes the ball at the bottom of its arc.

The longer shaft and flatter lie of the driver promote a more shallow downswing plane which allows the club head at the bottom of its arc to pass

Above: A sudden transition in swing speed by snatching with the hands forces the body to straighten during the downswing and encourages the wrists to uncock prematurely.

Above: If the hands do not exert any influence to control the downswing path and plane, the right side comes over the top. The left hand pulls the butt of the grip downwards with sufficient control to maintain the swing path.

horizontal to the ground and begin an upward arc as it strikes the ball.

As the hands, arms and body move in unison, the left hand continues pulling to create leverage and begin the process of squaring the club face to the back to the ball. This is achieved by merging the gradual uncocking of the wrists with a rotation of the back of the left hand and forearm. As the body continues to unwind and the weight is being transferred, pressure begins to

Above: The longer shaft and flatter lie of the driver promote a shallow downswing plane. Having initiated a pull to create leverage (above right) the left hand controls a gradual uncocking of the wrists in unison with a rotation of the left hand and forearm. Having gradually rotated during the backswing, they repeat the process during the downswing.

exert on to the left foot and leg. The outside of the foot resists this pressure while the lateral leg movement and unwinding hips simultaneously begin to pull the right foot counter-clockwise

The impact zone

Above: The sequence shows that as the body continues to unwind and the weight transfers, the club head returns from the inside on to the target line.

onto its toe and the path of the club head gradually returns to the target line.

The left side of the body clears, and the wrists uncock fully allowing the hands to deliver the club head to the ball. The role of the hands in the downswing is frequently misunderstood; the two most common errors are partly influenced by well meaning but erro-

Above: The role of the hands is often misunderstood, and golfers who are advised to hit with the right hand may force an early uncocking of the wrists.

neous advice. The attempt to 'hit it with the right hand' often results in the right hand passing under the left forcing an early uncocking of the wrists. An attempt to 'release or roll' the hands usually closes the face on to the ball at impact.

Practice drill

Without a club take your set up and position your left arm in its normal position with the palm open and the back of the hand facing the target. Swing the arm a short way back, altering the position of the left hand and forearm to simulate their position in a normal swing. Now simply let the arm swing down and feel it rotate (or unwind) to return the back of the hand to face the target at impact.

The drill simulates the function of timing the delivery and squaring the club face at impact. As the wrists uncock, the left forearm and left hand rotate in unison. This gradual rotation is timed to return the back of the hand during the drill (the club face in the actual swing) square with the ball and target line at the precise moment of impact, and not a moment before.

Below: Assume your set up with the left arm in its normal position and the back of the left hand facing the target. Rotate the left hand and forearm into their usual backswing position and let them unwind back to their original position.

The impact zone

Contrary to popular belief the right hand does not pass over the left which occurs if the body stops unwinding.

After impact the hands continue a rotation which occurs as a result of correct club head delivery and the body unwinding into the follow through.

A further piece of well meaning advice, which often proves counter-productive, is keeping the head down. If this is exaggerated, it can lead to a common driving error. As early as at the top of the backswing, the player who is conscious of keeping the head down tightens the neck muscles, thereby encouraging a hit at the ball. This, in turn, prevents the correct sequence of

Above: A conscious attempt at the top of the backswing to keep the head down will tighten the neck muscles and force you to hit at the ball, restricting follow through.

Above: After impact, as the body unwinds, the hands continue to rotate. However, they do not roll over.

downswing movement and extension through the ball.

The swing path, which has travelled from inside during the downswing back on to the target line at impact, then begins to travel back inside the line as both the hands and arms reach their maximum point of extension through impact. This is achieved because the body has not been restricted but allowed to continue unwinding. This allows the club head to continue through a maximum width of arc into the follow through. It is these two aspects, a freely unwinding body and maximum radius through the ball, which gradually pull the head to turn and look upwards during the throughswing.

As your hands and arms reach a point parallel with the ground the arms begin to fold; simultaneously the body completes its unwinding process and pulls the right foot around completely on to its toe to fully transfer the weight. As the arms complete the fold, the hands finish by the side of the head with the club lying behind the head, and the trunk facing the target.

As the hands and arms reach maximum extension, the swing path travels inside the line. As your hands extend through to a horizontal position, the arms begin to fold. As the body completes its unwinding, the right foot is pulled on to the toes. The hands finish to the side of the head with the trunk facing the target.

CHAPTER SIX

Power

Jim Christine

If you asked a number of golfers what they were seeking most in their golf game, a very high percentage would answer that they wanted more distance in their tee shots. Most people would love a few extra yards on their drives. They see this as being a very important step to lower scores. This idea is probably correct, as the game of golf does become a little easier the nearer you are to the green, so long driving must be of great benefit.

This means that the development of power is a very important area of the game. Indeed, the only reason you take a swing at all is to develop power, as it must be regarded as the main function of the swing. But what is power in a golf swing? What makes one player able to propel the ball so much further than another? These are the first questions that you must address before you can go on to think of how to generate that power.

The answer to these questions must lie back in the science laboratory at school. Force (power) is directly measurable; it is directly linked to the size of an object (mass) and the speed at which that object is moving (speed). In golfing terms, the mass is set for us, i.e. the size and weight of the club head; this does not change greatly. Therefore, the factor that changes must be the speed. It is true to say that the faster the club head is moving when it impacts the ball, the further that ball will go. Club head speed holds the key to the distance the ball will fly. This is what constitutes power in a golf swing!

Clearly, it is essential to introduce a few ground rules at this stage. Otherwise, after the last sweeping statement, you would be quite justified in thinking that it would be acceptable to take a run at the ball from a distance, thereby generating a tremendous amount of club head speed. This may well be the method you would employ if you were given 10 shots to produce the longest drive you could. However, this is not what golf demands from you. You have got to be consistent in your striking, and therefore out-and-out power generation has to be tempered with accuracy in order to play successful golf. I will go on to deal with accuracy in greater detail in a later chapter, but do bear in mind as you progress with your development of power, that the demands of accuracy will always need to be considered.

Power

The development of power

I would like you to think of the development of power in your golf swing as a similar function to developing power in a throwing action. In the photos below, I am using only my arm to generate power and therefore could only expect to throw the ball to a reasonably close target. However, in the photo opposite, I have definitely begun to generate more power by using my body as well as my arm.

This gives a vital clue to the generation of power in any physical movement. As the largest muscles available lie in the body and legs, the generation of your maximum power must start with your body action. This power is then conveyed through your smaller muscles,

adding in their own power at the same time to finally produce the maximum. It is a chain reaction, dependent on every muscle doing its job to produce the final product. The power production in your golf swing is exactly the same, only you have an extra dimension, your driver, multiplying that power still further.

The throwing action can be of further help in deciding what the correct body action during a golf swing should be. It is clear from the position shown opposite that I have taken my

body weight back on to my right foot. This is indeed what you will see in any throwing action. At the end of a throwing movement, you will also see that the vast majority of the body weight ends up on the forward foot. This weight transference is a very important part of power generation and therefore must take place in your golf swing.

In the photographic sequence on page 76 you will see how this weight

Above: Weight back, weight through: the classic movement in a throwing action. This weight transference is important in your golf swing.

transfer takes place in your swing. It is essentially a rotary movement, turning your body weight back on to your right foot in the backswing and forward on to your left foot in the follow through. This is often described as the 'body pivot'. Let us look at it in more detail.

75

Power

The body pivot

In the set up, the body weight is fairly evenly distributed between the feet, perhaps just slightly more on the right foot. As the pivot begins, the right shoulder turns back, moving the body weight little by little more on to the right foot. At the end of the backswing pivot the shoulders should have turned through 90 degrees, and 75 per cent of the body weight is on the right foot. The hip turn has been kept to the minimum required to achieve this 90-degree shoulder turn and, as you can see, the flex in the right knee has been maintained. Both the restriction of the hip turn and the position of the right knee help to create the coiling of the upper body against the lower, which is essential for the production of power.

At the start of the downswing, the body weight should be allowed to flow smoothly back towards the left foot until it is back to the even distribution of the set up. Now the left shoulder will turn to the left, bringing the body weight through to the left foot until the final position is reached, with the vast majority of the body weight, some 90 per cent or more, on the left foot. This body pivot is a key source of power in your golf swing!

Opposite: This sequence shows the body pivot: the heart of a good golf swing. Right: Halfway back and the spinal angle has remained constant – all is well here.

Power

The arm swing

The arm swing must now develop what power it can to add to the power of the body pivot. The power available to the arm swing comes through the building up and use of leverage. Once again, thinking back to the throwing action will be of some help here. Imagine trying to throw a ball without using your elbow or wrist. It would be impossible to generate any speed of movement, and therefore it would also be impossible to throw the ball any

distance. The same principle applies to your golf swing. Swing with your arms absolutely straight, and you will not move the ball very far at all. The role of your arm swing in the creation of power is to develop what leverage it can and then make the best use of it during the striking of the ball.

Look at the backswing position in the photograph above. Although a great deal of effort had been put in, very little angle has appeared in the right elbow or in the wrists. Little leverage has been created here, and if the forward swing was made from this position, no power would be achieved.

In the arm swing for maximum power, an angle of 90 degrees should be

Above left: Little leverage has been developed here and therefore no power is available. Above: This shows maximum leverage just after the start of the downswing.

achieved between the left arm and the club shaft on the backswing. At the beginning of the downswing this angle should increase slightly as the wrists react to the weight of the club.

Left: Power is passed on if some leverage is left intact at impact. Above: However, all the power is lost if this is the impact!

Some of this leverage should still be maintained right up to impact. As you can see, the club head lags a little behind the hands, making sure that the club will still be accelerating, and thereby helping you to create those few extra yards.

This is leverage at its best, developed in the backswing, stored in the first part of the downswing, and released to best effect through the ball. Compare this to the position in the photograph above: the club head has passed the hands before the strike which means that the club must have been slowing down at impact – death to achieving good distance from the tee.

Leverage from the arm swing is a priority source of power in your golf swing. Just for a moment, take a look at

Power

the photograph below. This is quite different. The collapsing of the left elbow has actually produced more leverage, but it is doubtful if this can be used consistently, once again making the point that there has to be a tempering of power in order to retain accuracy. This is leverage at its best, developed on the backswing and stored for use during the strike!

Arc width

This is often talked about in relation to power and, as mentioned in the equip-

Right: There is lots of power here, but will the golfer get back to the ball?

ment section, lengthening the shaft of the club, which would result in a wider arc, will produce extra yards. However, as far as the swing is concerned, the length of the left arm created the arc width, and as long as that arm remains comfortably straight throughout the swing until shortly after impact, no more can be expected from arc width with regard to increased power.

Arc length

It is correct to say that the longer the swing the longer the arc would be. This does have potential for increased speed due to the opportunity of accelerating the club for a longer period of time before impact takes place. This again creates the problems shown opposite. The return journey to the ball from here will be too difficult to strike the ball accurately on a consistent basis. Therefore, although a longer swing arc would provide the opportunity of increased power, most players would find a very long swing too difficult to control.

Swing speed

Swing speed, without doubt, will affect the distance the ball will fly. Once you are able to perform efficiently the moves outlined earlier, the faster you are able to do them, and whilst retaining your efficiency, the longer your shots will become. However, there will always be a trade-off between speed creating power and power creating length of shot and the increase in speed with which usually comes a decrease in accuracy. This is an equation you will always be trying to balance.

Passing on the power

This is a subject we have already just touched on, but it is a very important one. In order to pass on efficiently the power you have generated, you have to hit the middle of the ball with the middle of the club. A one-inch move away from this centred strike costs you approximately 25 yards in distance. This seems to be a good time to move on to examining accuracy, which is detailed in the next chapter.

These two photos show a solid strike and a good shot (above), and one inch off centre (left)!

81

CHAPTER SEVEN

Accuracy

Jim Christine

You will have already gone a long way to developing accurate driving if you have worked diligently through the set-up section. No-one has ever produced consistently accurate golf shots with a poor grip or a bad position at the ball. It is essential to your further progress that you practise your set-up procedures in order to provide the sound foundations required on which you can build an accurate golf swing.

If you look at a picture of a swinging rope, it is easy to see that as long as the centre of the swing remains constant, the end of the rope will describe a consistent circle. Well, imagine that your club head is tracing a path as you swing it around your body. This path is called the 'swing arc' and, although it cannot be circular, it is necessary to make it as consistent a shape as possible. The key to an accurate swing is to produce a consistent swing arc!

Above: In a centred swinging motion, centrifugal force will help maintain an accurate swing arc.

Look at the movement shown in the swing sequence on pages 84-85. Although it is obviously a movement of great power, it is well balanced from start to finish. The movements flow smoothly together, and every part of the swing has come together in one cohesive unit. This is the consistent swing required for accuracy, quite different to some that I have seen and, I am sure, to some that you have seen too.

If you cannot maintain your own position and balance throughout the swing, how can you expect the club's arc to be maintained? Any loss of balance during your swing may not have resulted in a bad shot last time, but it soon will. In order to produce accuracy you must have control of your movements, and that is what you will learn from this section.

Accuracy

The swing

As this photographic sequence shows, in a good, accurate swing no one part can play an over-dominant role. Look at the overall movement and appreciate how well it all flows together. This is what you are seeking to achieve through your practice and training.

Accuracy

The body pivot

Your body pivot must be used to provide accuracy. It must play the very important role of giving the swing arc its centre. This cannot be an absolute centre around your head, as many people believe, as this would result in a movement with no weight transfer. An absolute fixed centre would provide you with the most consistent arc there is, no doubt, but, as you are aware, the weight transfer is an essential part of the generation of power, so a compromise must be reached in this area. In fact, your golf swing is a two-axis movement, one for the backswing and one for the downswing and follow through. This movement will create an elliptical arc with which it will be possible to become extremely accurate.

The next stage is to attempt to make sure that your swing arc always returns to the correct level. It would be no good if you were hitting two inches behind the ball one minute, then missing the ball by swinging above it the next. This area of your swing is again controlled by your body pivot, this time by maintaining your spinal angle. So you can see that for accuracy your body pivot must:

1 Provide a consistent two-axis pivot.
2 Maintain the spinal angle throughout the pivot.

Let's look at these two factors in more detail.

Above right: The centred body weight is too short. Right: At the end of the backswing pivot, approximately 75 per cent of the body weight is on the right foot.

The two-axis pivot

Look at the picture sequence. As you can see, a golf club shaft has been positioned on either side of the body, and this will help to demonstrate the body pivot more clearly.

In the set up, the body weight is positioned reasonably centrally, perhaps just slightly more on the right foot. But as the backswing takes place, more of the body weight is being moved on to the right foot. By the end of the backswing approximately 75 per cent is being carried on the right foot. The swing has moved back into the right axis. As the downswing begins, the body weight is moved smoothly back towards the left foot, and the left axis has been formed.

Compare the photo below with the opposite photo (top). Can you see the subtle difference? In the picture opposite, there is an obvious gap between the left golf club shaft and the left hip and leg. In the photo below (left), the left leg and hip are just beginning to touch that shaft. Clearly there is a difference. That difference is caused by the slight majority of your body weight just reaching your left foot prior to impact. With that left axis established, the left side turns, keeping the whole body just inside the line of the shaft by the end of the movement. This is a perfect example of a two-axis body pivot controlling the body weight, creating a base on which to build good swing arc control.

Far left: At impact, the slight majority of the body weight just favours the left foot with the left hip just touching the shaft. Left: At the end of the movement, 90 per cent of the body weight is on the left foot with the body just resting against the shaft.

Accuracy

Beware of the disastrous movement that often occurs when too much emphasis is placed on the 'keep your head down' theory of body pivoting. The weight is moved to the right in the backswing, and therefore as the backswing is finished more weight is actually on the left foot. Then, even after a huge effort is made, the body weight cannot continue moving forwards throughout the downswing. Finally, the upper body becomes trapped, the weight stays on the right foot until the end of the swing and you have the disastrous 'reverse weight transfer', which is the cause of many poor shots. So if you hear the phrase 'Keep your head down', just ignore it!

Below: The dreaded reverse pivot. At the end of the backswing movement the weight favours the left foot. At the end of the follow through the weight favours the right foot. This is death to power and accuracy.

Key tip

Just a word of warning on the two-axis pivot. Do not exaggerate the movement; remember that you must stay inside the area depicted by the two golf club shafts, or you will have no hope of producing consistent accurate shots.

Sometimes good points can be exaggerated. Do not allow the body to sway – it is impossible to be consistent from this position.

Accuracy

Maintain the spine angle

Now look at the body pivot from a different direction, down the line. The spinal angle is created at set up during the taking up of your posture position. The spinal column has been tilted forward from the hips forming an angle between the top of your spine and your hips, and your hips and feet. This is called the *spine angle* and it has to be maintained through the majority of your swing, certainly at least until the

Above: The start of the body pivot from the down the line position. Note the spinal angle.

Right: Nearing the end of the backswing movement: check that the spinal angle has remained the same as at set up and that the right knee has retained its flex.

ball has been struck, if consistently accurate contact is to be achieved. As you can see from the photographs, the spine angle has been maintained, making sure that the distance from the player's throat to the ball has remained

The end of the impact zone shows the spine angle still constant and the weight moving smoothly through to the left foot.

Above: At impact, keep the spine angle constant and feel the slight majority of weight (60 per cent) favouring the left foot.

constant. This is the purpose of maintaining the spine angle, and the second function that the body pivot provides for building a consistent swing arc.

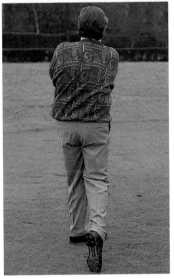

Left: The end of the movement: the body weight has moved almost fully through to the left foot and the spine angle is finally released to ease the strain on the player's back.

Accuracy

The arm swing

The function of the arm swing in the creation of accuracy is to position the club in the correct relationship to the body pivot throughout the swing. It would not be sensible to go to all the time and trouble of creating a stable

Left and above: The relationship between the arms and the body is a very close one in a correct golf swing. Once this relationship has been established at set up, it is extremely important not to place too much pressure on it throughout the entire swing movement.

body pivot only to then allow the arms and hands to move completely independently of this. The arm swing must be linked to the body pivot creating one cohesive unit of movement, thus providing consistent, accurate shots.

Your left arm has a big role to play in this area of the swing. If you can keep it at a consistent length during the swing this will provide a very consistent

arc. This idea was first introduced to many people as 'keeping your left arm straight'. Indeed this is a very good concept, but unfortunately it has the tendency to breed swings that are full of tension. Players take too literally the idea of straightness and produce a very stiff left arm, restricting their movement and producing very poor golf swings. You must stay with the concept of maintaining the width of the arc with your

Driving

In this sequence look at how the arm swing complements the body pivot. There is no argument between them – just a sense of everything working together.

Accuracy

left arm, but see it as tension free, rather than rigid and locked at the elbow.

In the swing sequence you can appreciate that the left arm has done its job of maintaining the width of the swing arc. Take a good close look at the elbow; at first sight it looks very straight, but on close inspection it appears to have a soft, slightly bowed look. This is the correct arm tension during the swing. The swinging weight of the club will help you to maintain your arc width without the need for a huge amount of tension in your left arm. You must not allow your arm to collapse. This would not be a route to accuracy, but remember to keep your left arm tension free.

Below: The left arm provides a consistent radius to the swing arc. Keep it relaxed as any tension will cause poor mobility and will undermine your attempt to produce a fluid, rhythmical movement.

Rhythm

The rhythm of your swing is the final link which must keep everything working together. Rhythms can be fast or slow: there have been great players with either style. But there is no mistaking the fact that great golfers always have good rhythm. Nick Price would possibly be the first player to enter your mind as a modern example of a fast rhythm; Seve Ballesteros has the silky-smooth rhythm everyone envies when he is in full flight and at his best. Nick Faldo, the best player in the world today, is blessed with great rhythm; his swing is both a technical and rhythmical joy to watch. Rhythm is the look that all great sportsmen and women show when, even in moments of great stress, they appear to have all the time in the world to perform the task they are required to perform. This is the secret of rhythm: to give yourself time. There should be no snatched, hurried movements, no great surges of acceleration, in an attempt to whack the ball a huge distance. In moments of stress, in the heat of battle out there on the course, give yourself time. Swing smoothly, keep your movements together. This is rhythm, your final key to unlock the door of long, accurate driving.

These photos show positions, but you must remember that there are no positions in a swinging movement! You should keep your mind clear and feel your swing as one continuous movement. 'Feel' is the key to good driving and is largely due to the rhythm you develop in your swing.

CHAPTER EIGHT

Driving strategy

Nick Allen

How many times have you heard golfers complain about the unimpressive ball striker who always manages to get the ball round in lower scores than his playing partners? Next time you play, analyse how your round was affected by position from the tee. Driving into fairway hazards; second shots restricted through poor position off the tee; driving into trees or out of bounds; you cannot capitalize on acquiring sound technique unless it is related to an understanding of sound playing strategy.

A common error is the complacency that many golfers show on their home course. They fail to learn the strategic distances between tees and hazards, and this undermines their game plan. Conversely, when visiting new courses their preparation and general shot management is often better.

On analysis you may be surprised to learn that in addition to dropping shots through poor technique, a large percentage of dropped shots are caused through failing to establish a sound game plan, one that can be adapted to changing weather conditions. Use the following programme as a basis to organise your playing approach at your home course.

Driving strategy

Home course approach

The first key to sound strategy from the tee is to establish your average and maximum driving distances. The ideal place for this exercise is a practice range at a golf course. It is important that you use the same type of ball that you normally play with, approximately 30 balls are sufficient.

Establish the yardage

If you are working from an existing yardage book, it is important to establish the exact point from where the yardage was taken, or if you are pacing or using a wheel yourself, start the measurement from the fixed plate. This is important so that you can add or subtract distance for daily tee changes; a tee moved back from a position where you would normally hit a 3 wood may now allow you to hit the driver. Conversely, if it is moved forward, you may be required to use an iron.

Tee changes often bring into play otherwise redundant hazards, and establishing a fixed yardage point will allow you to make the necessary adjustments for distance.

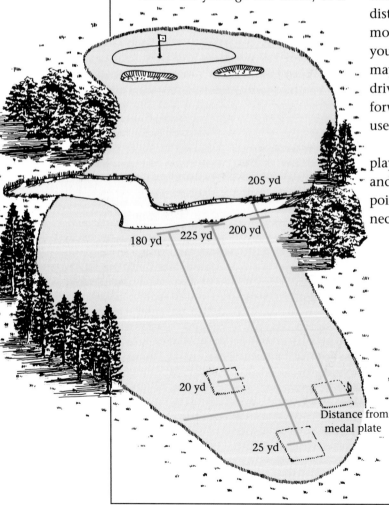

205 yd

180 yd 225 yd 200 yd

20 yd

Distance from medal plate

25 yd

You can determine the distance from the fixed yardage plate to the front and rear of the hazard. On days when the positions vary, you should pace off the distance and add or subtract accordingly for accurate judgement.

Plan ahead on par 5s

Golfers often get complacent when playing wide fairways where any hazards are not within range of the drive. The tee shot is often hit aimlessly on the basis that there are not any fairway hazards to challenge it. A par 5 hole, for example, may be designed to chal- lenge the second shot. The line from the tee may involve a degree of risk, driving close to a line of trees or a boundary fence with a reward of a feasible angle to the green for the second shot. Con- versely, if the player chooses the wider margin for error, the second shot option may be severely limited.

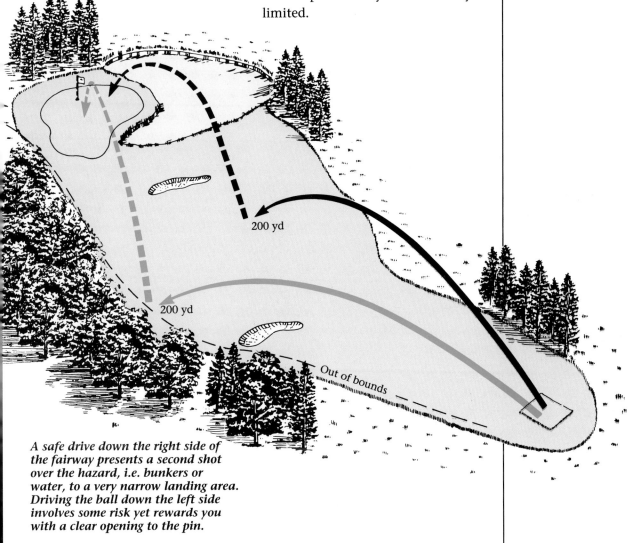

200 yd

200 yd

Out of bounds

A safe drive down the right side of the fairway presents a second shot over the hazard, i.e. bunkers or water, to a very narrow landing area. Driving the ball down the left side involves some risk yet rewards you with a clear opening to the pin.

Driving strategy

Plan ahead on par 4s

From a good tee shot a short par 4 may require only an approach to the green from 140 yards, where similarly the wide fairway appears to offer many options for the shot to the green. However, the green may be guarded by water or sand and angled in such a way that it will receive a shot only from a particular point on the fairway.

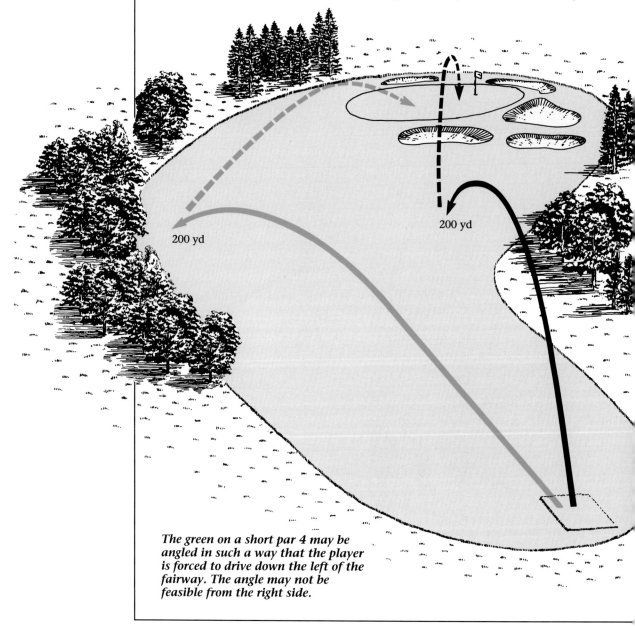

200 yd

200 yd

The green on a short par 4 may be angled in such a way that the player is forced to drive down the left of the fairway. The angle may not be feasible from the right side.

Practice drill

Mark each ball with ink or use the identification numbers on the balls so that you can list their striking order. This allows you to note after each shot the feel of the swing and whether the swing speed was 100 per cent or controlled.

After a few trials a pattern will emerge which will identify your average and maximum distance. The test must be made in windless conditions and on a level fairway. Continue testing to determine your driving distance with a 3 wood or 1 iron and the 2 iron. If your course has a yardage book, memorize the distances between the medal tees and hazards. If not, then work out how many normal paces you take to 100 yards and pace the distance or, preferably, use a yardage wheel.

Fairway contours

A short par 4 may have a change in fairway contours which places a degree of difficulty on the second shot from a long drive. The player has to decide whether to play from a level lie albeit a longer approach, whether he is capable of driving through the change in gradient on to level ground, or whether to play the shot from the difficult lie.

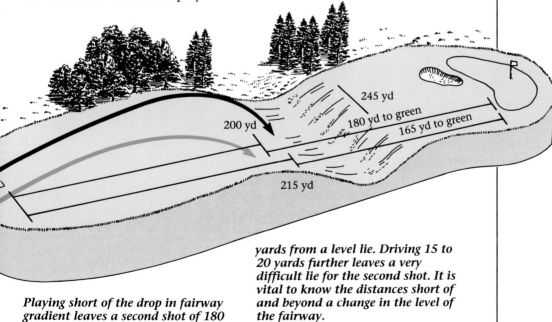

245 yd

180 yd to green

200 yd

165 yd to green

215 yd

Playing short of the drop in fairway gradient leaves a second shot of 180 yards from a level lie. Driving 15 to 20 yards further leaves a very difficult lie for the second shot. It is vital to know the distances short of and beyond a change in the level of the fairway.

Driving strategy

Dog-leg holes

On dog-leg holes there are four vital yardages that you must know: firstly the distance to carry the corner of the dog-leg, especially if you are a long hitter; the minimum distance you need to drive the ball to gain complete access into the second part of the dog-leg; on your approach shot, which part of the fairway to play to; and, finally, the 'run out' distance at the far corner of the dog-leg.

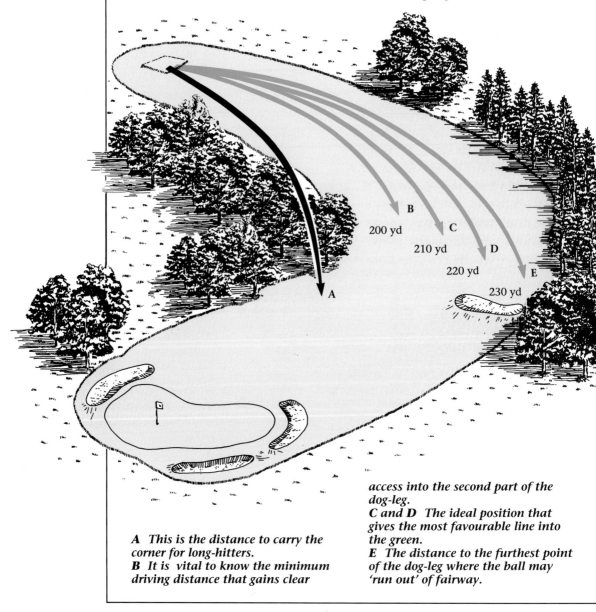

200 yd
210 yd
220 yd
230 yd

A This is the distance to carry the corner for long-hitters.
B It is vital to know the minimum driving distance that gains clear access into the second part of the dog-leg.
C and D The ideal position that gives the most favourable line into the green.
E The distance to the furthest point of the dog-leg where the ball may 'run out' of fairway.

The effect of wind

Wind obviously has a strong influence and must be taken into account when deciding strategy from the tee. This includes its effect down wind of reaching hazards otherwise not in range, and where it might affect the carry of traps which do not usually warrant concern.

Side winds also require careful consideration; a well struck shot on the correct line can move a significant distance in a strong side wind. On a narrow tree-lined fairway a drive hit down the middle may not hold the fairway in a side wind.

Wind affecting distance

Strong winds can bring otherwise redundant hazards into play, so make sure that you know the distance to traps that are not usually in play. When playing into a strong wind, a trap position at 195 yards may be difficult to carry. Conversely, one at 260 yards may be reachable down wind.

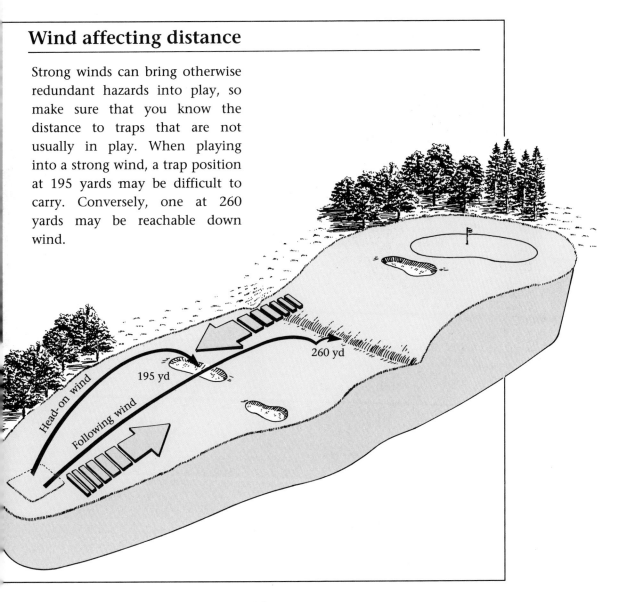

260 yd

195 yd

Head-on wind

Following wind

Driving strategy

Side winds

The ideal line for the second shot may require a drive down the middle of the fairway. It may be difficult to avoid the right-hand traps in a strong left-to-right wind (**A**). Although the second shot from the left side (**B**) is more difficult, it provides the better option in these conditions.

A
200 yd

B
200 yd

Wind

Choosing a teeing area

The tee shot provides you with an opportunity to select a position from which to play, yet many players tee the ball carelessly and sometimes give themselves an uneven lie. Not all teeing areas are level and positioning the ball in the fairway is a vital start to the hole. Remember that you are allowed to tee the ball two club lengths behind the line of the tee markers.

When teeing off out of a funnel of trees, look for overhanging branches that could catch your shot and tee the ball on the favourable side.

Many golfers tee the ball exactly between the two tee markers, often coming close to infringing the Rules. Remember that you can select where you tee the ball within a rectangle formed by the line between the tee markers and two club lengths in depth (even if you stand outside it). This is important when finding a level stance.

Driving strategy

Club selection considerations

Once you have established your range of distance with the driver, 3 wood and long irons, and analysed the strategic distances shown, you will have the information that provides a basis for selecting woods versus irons from the tee. These principles are fundamental in club selection, but there are some additional considerations, and it is impor-tant to recognise the underlying objective of the round so that you can react according to various situations that can unfold.

In a medal qualifying round when nothing extra can be gained from shooting the lowest score, your objective should be to qualify. On the final few holes, it is not often that you know the qualifying score, although occasionally if you have a late tee time you may become aware of this. Sometimes instinct tells you how well you are doing. If you find yourself in this situa-

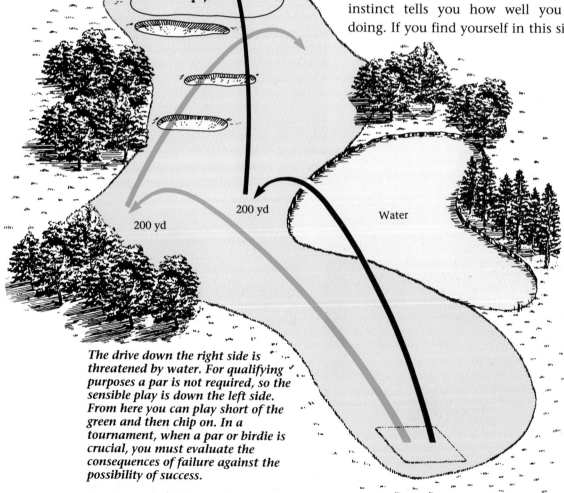

200 yd

200 yd

Water

The drive down the right side is threatened by water. For qualifying purposes a par is not required, so the sensible play is down the left side. From here you can play short of the green and then chip on. In a tournament, when a par or birdie is crucial, you must evaluate the consequences of failure against the possibility of success.

tion and the finishing holes offer a small margin for error on the drive, the consequences of attempting to find an ideal position from the tee and missing may ruin your score. In this situation it is far better to play to a safe zone and concede a dropped shot.

In a tournament medal round the situation may be different, and you may be aware that a par or birdie is required. In this situation, confidence plays an important part, and you must decide whether to risk the consequences of failure for the possibility of success.

It may involve driving the ball to a narrow part of the fairway, or attempting to carry the ball over a hazard usually regarded as out of reach.

Plan your playing strategy

We all know that confidence and swing feel are both very changeable, and you may find it necessary to modify your normal playing strategy. If you have missed a few fairways from the tee, then even on wide fairways you can restore your confidence by using a 3 wood or an iron from the tee to get the ball in play.

In a medal round, if your playing partner becomes your direct contender,

Playing a medal round

If your partner becomes your closest contender in a medal round, play your drive short so that you can play first to the green and apply some pressure. If you are unsure of the second shot, play your drive longer to learn from your partner.

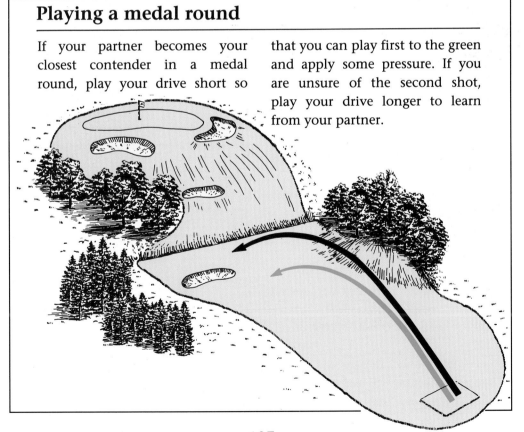

Driving strategy

drive the ball short so that you can play the approach first and then put the pressure on – the same principle applies in matchplay. Conversely, if you are uncertain of the second shot and how the ball may react when it lands on the green, play your tee shot longer and learn from your partner/opponent's shot.

The emphasis that modern course designers place on the strategic placement of hazards requires golfers to plan their playing strategy carefully. Having safely positioned a difficult tee shot it is not uncommon to find that your approach to the green must negotiate

Although the club face loft of a long iron and fairway wood may be similar, when viewed from the player's position the profile of a wood often instills greater confidence. It is easier to use because of the different design function of the sole.

strategic sand and water placement. A sound technique with fairway woods will prove invaluable, particularly with regard to the length of new course developments.

For men and women, the choice between using a fairway wood or a long iron is extremely important, yet too

often it is based on conforming to a false logic where golfers feel that using the long iron is a sign of a better player. In certain circumstances the fairway wood can offer a greater margin for error where to persist with a long iron could adversely affect your score.

Although the standard loft of a 5 wood is close to that of a 2 iron (22 degrees and 20 degrees respectively), the design and function of the long iron at impact require more precision from the player. During the set up, when looking down at a long iron or a wood even with identical face loft, most players favour the wood. The profile of a thin blade and narrow sole often induces a lack of

Key tip

You can improve your strategy and game plan at your home course by testing your range of distances with fairway woods and establishing at each hole the distance from where your drives usually finish to each hazard in the fairway, and forward to the front of the green.

On this par 5, the second shot is played to position in preparation for a third pitch shot on to the green.

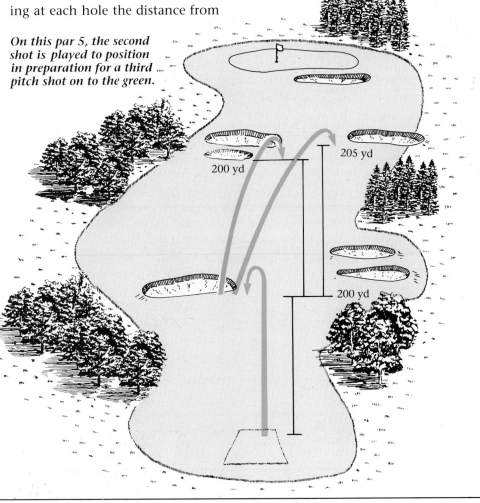

confidence which forces the player to mistime his swing and manipulate the ball into the air. Conversely, the profile of a wood with its wider sole serves to promote confidence.

To achieve the timing and the precise delivery of club head to ball it is essential to grip the club correctly.

The longer shaft and lie angle of the fairway wood will establish your posture and distance from the ball. This, in turn, will influence the swing path and plane, which also affect the delivery of the club head to the ball.

CHAPTER NINE

Swing faults

Nick Allen

Often a player's ball striking ability is not reflected accurately in their handicap. Learning to lower your score requires a combination of factors: firstly, a basic skill element in each aspect of golf linked with an awareness for sound playing strategy. For example, a player who is proficient in the majority of skill aspects, except perhaps for bunker play or long irons, frequently ruins a good round when called upon to execute these shots. It is therefore important to acquire a basic understanding of swing technique, so that when problems arise you can search for the remedy.

In the following sequence of driving errors you will be able to trace a chain of faults from their root cause through to impact. Refer to these fault sequences as a systematic approach to working on your game.

Swing faults

Topping

Topping the ball with the driver is the most common fault that beginners encounter. One of the most common causes of a topped shot is lifting your head, but there are also many other contributing factors as detailed below.

Standing too far from the ball

This is a common fault among beginners. It is important to establish the correct distance from the ball at address which enables you to maintain weight distribution and balance during the swing. When a player reaches for the ball with too much weight on the toes at address, instinctively the posture will straighten during the backswing shifting weight backwards on to the heels.

Conversely, some players reach for the ball with the weight sitting back on the heels, and as the swing starts the weight moves forwards towards the toes.

Above: Reaching for the ball at address can cause the player to straighten to maintain stability, thereby forcing the weight back on to the heels.

Above and right: Too much weight on the heels at address can have the opposite effect of moving the weight on to the toes as the downswing begins.

We are often given the well-meaning advice to 'sit' and bend our knees but this can create poor posture and causes the player to straighten during the downswing.

This instability can cause the trunk to straighten during the downswing or force the player to snatch the club.

Your posture at address sets the foundation to the swing, and many golfers concentrate merely on flexing the knees and not on establishing the important body angle at address. The image of 'sitting down' and flexing the knees often creates a rounded back and crouching position at address. This often feels comfortable to the player, particularly as the driver is the longest club in the bag. However, a wide and more shallow swing plane with the driver cannot be initiated from a crouched posture, and during the downswing the player increases height through impact to accommodate the length of the club.

Swing faults

Moving weight on to the right side

As the swing starts, another common fault is to move the weight quickly across to the right side, causing the shoulders to tilt steeply. This can cause the left arm to collapse at the top of the backswing. The hands 'cast' the club to start the downswing, forcing the weight on to the right leg at impact.

If the club travels too quickly on an inside path, it can cause the right knee to straighten, allowing the hips to turn excessively; this moves the weight into the left side at the top of the backswing. As the club approaches impact the weight rapidly moves on to the right leg as the right side spins out.

Above: The hips have moved laterally forcing the hands to lift the club early into a steep plane. The left arm starts to collapse the width of arc and the weight moves to the right.

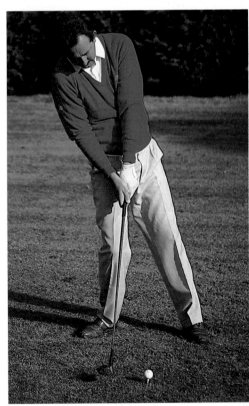

Above and right: If the club travels too quickly inside the line or the right knee straightens, the excessive hip turn forces weight into the left side at the top. The right side then comes over the top to dominate the downswing.

Practice drill

To establish the correct posture, stand with your trunk erect and extend your arms with the club shaft parallel with the ground. Retain a slight flex in the knees. Bend slowly forwards from the waist maintaining the knee flex until the club is grounded.

Above and top: As the hands approach hip height the wrists cock gradually, blending with the motion of the backswing.

The swing unit formed by the hands, arms and shoulders starts the club away from the ball, and simultaneously the left side of the body begins to turn. As the hands approach hip height, an even weight distribution is maintained resulting from the pivotal turn. At this point the width of arc has been

Above: The wrist cock has established maximum width of arc. At the top, a greater proportion of weight is on the right.

Swing faults

established, and it is maintained during the backswing from a gradual wrist set while the body continues turning.

At the top of the backswing, a greater proportion of the weight is positioned into the right side. As the weight begins to transfer during the downswing, the left hand pulls to control the uncocking of the wrists and time the club head delivery. The wrists uncock slightly earlier with the driver than with an iron, allowing the club head to pass above the ground at the bottom of the arc and contact the ball slightly on the upswing. From the rear you can see the shallower swing plane formed by the posture at address and the lie of the club.

Above: The left hand controls a gradual uncocking of the wrists and allows the club head to descend from a shallow angle, passing horizontal to the ground before sweeping the ball away. Right: The posture at address and the longer driver shaft and flatter lie influence the desired swing.

Skying

The ball position with the driver dictates the club head's angle of attack and the ball's subsequent flight trajectory and distance. A ball positioned too far back in the stance does not allow the wrists to uncock in time; consequently the club head angle on to the ball is too steep and this often results in a skyed shot if the ball is contacted by the top edge of the club face.

A player with an excessively strong grip will break the wrists very early in the backswing creating an acute angle between the left arm and club shaft,

Above and right: A ball positioned too far back in the stance will not allow the wrist cock to recover in time during the downswing. The angle of attack is too steep, and the ball is struck on the top edge of the club face causing a skyed shot.

Swing faults

which never recovers in the downswing. The hands lead the club head, again causing a steep angle of attack.

During the downswing if the weight shifts on to the left side too

Right: A strong grip at address encourages an early wrist break. The wrists cannot uncock in time and the hands are forced to lead the club head, decreasing club face loft at impact.

quickly, the body blocks the hands and arms and the wrists cannot uncock in time. Lifting the left heel too far off the ground encourages too much flexibility in the hips, and this can lead to a reverse

pivot. While the usual instinct is to spin back to the right side, quite often the player swings the hands and arms down fast, forcing the body ahead of the ball. The hands lead the club head to such an extent that the left arm buckles through impact, and the steep angle again produces a skyed shot.

Left and above: The weight moves into the left side too early in the downswing, restricting the passage of the arms and hands. Lifting the left heel or straightening the right knee gives the hips too much freedom. This can reverse pivot the weight into the left side at the top. A snatch down forces the body to trap the through swing and the left arm buckles.

Pre-shot routine

The ball is positioned just inside the left heel for the driver, and this simple pre-shot routine will avoid the error of positioning it too far back in the stance.

Place the right foot slightly behind the line of the ball as you ground the club head (left foot is pulled to a position behind the right heel). Slide the left foot into position

Above: As you put the right foot into position at right angles to the target line slightly behind the ball line, move the left foot into position, then the right.

slightly wide of the ball, and then move the right foot into its final position.

Neutralize your grip if it is too strong. Hold the butt end of the grip between the thumb and forefinger of

Above and right: Hold the butt of the grip between your right thumb and forefinger, placing an open palmed left hand against the grip.

your right hand and place your left hand against the side of the grip to ensure correct placement; two knuckles should be visible as you look down the line between the thumb and forefinger pointing between your chin and right shoulder. Overlap or interlock the small finger, making sure that the grip lies through the fingers of the right hand. Close the pad of the right thumb over the left thumb; both 'V's should point between the chin and right shoulder.

Make sure that the line between the thumb and forefinger of the left hand points between the chin and right shoulder. The grip should run through the fingers of the right hand, allowing the right pad to close over the left thumb.

Swing faults

Controlling weight distribution

The purpose of the turn in the backswing is two-fold: it allows the hands and arms to swing the club head uninhibitedly and to maintain maximum width of arc. It is also the major contributory power source on the swing. To control your weight distribution, which affects the delivery of the club head, you should practise the following simple exercise.

Practice drill

Form your posture and cross your arms against your chest facing a mirror. Imagine that your spine represents your swing centre and simply lish the necessary width of arc with the driver to enable you to execute a timed recovery and deliver the club head on the correct arc.

Above: If your hands, arms and shoulders move in unison with the turn, you can achieve a good weight distribution and maintain the maximum width of arc.

practise pivoting your body around this centre to simulate your backswing turn. At the top you can see the angle on which the shoulders turn and how the right knee has retained its flex. If your turn functions correctly at the start of the swing and the swing unit (hands, arms and shoulders) moves in unison, you will control the weight distribution during the swing. You will also estab-

Above: Cross your arms on your chest and visualize your spine as a fixed axis or swing centre. Practise the pivotal body turn.

Poor flight trajectory and lack of distance

The efforts of many golfers to keep the ball in play and control accuracy often lead to poor flight trajectory and lack of distance. The player subdues uncocking the wrists in the downswing thereby preventing the hands from controlling the club face correctly through impact.

A strong grip at address, or positioning the hands too far forward, often leads to an early wrist break which establishes an acute angle between the left arm and club shaft. The hands lead the club head in the downswing preventing the wrists from uncocking completely; through impact the hands and club face are prevented from rotating and the club face is held square

A strong grip or hands too far forward at address lead to an early wrist break setting an acute angle between the left arm and club shaft. The wrists cannot recover in the downswing and the hands lead the club head at impact, decreasing club face loft.

Swing faults

through impact to steer the ball. This contrived action restricts the proper weight transference and club head speed. It also reduces the dynamic club face loft at impact to produce a low flight with a short carry.

Quite often the player will address the ball with a perfect grip and set up yet close the club face during the back-

Above: During the takeaway, the club face gradually opens in time with the turn, and as the wrists approach hip height they begin to set.

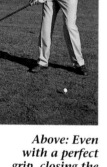

Above: Even with a perfect grip, closing the club head at takeaway encourages the hands to lead the club head through impact.

swing. The hands lead again through impact resisting the natural rotation that should take place. Check that the 'V' formed between the thumb and forefinger on the left hand points between your chin and right shoulder. The grip should lie through the fingers of your right hand so that the pad of your right

thumb can close in a comfortable position on top of your left thumb. When you ground the club, the position in which you set your hands in relation to the club head is vital and will affect how you time club head delivery. At address the hands should be level with the club head; this ensures that the correct club face loft is presented to the ball. During the takeaway allow the club face to gradually open in time with your turn; this activates a gradual setting of the wrists as your hands reach waist height.

Practice drill

Stand on a mat or carpet in front of a mirror and observe how your wrists uncock as you slowly simulate the downswing. As the hands rotate to square the club face at impact, they are realigned with the

club head (as they were at address), and the correct dynamic club face loft has been presented to the ball.

The swing speed as the club head is delivered to the ball will ensure a natural hand and club face rotation through impact.

Hooking

Usually when we first take hold of a golf club, what appears to be a comfortable and instinctive way to grip is, what we later discover, called a strong, or a hooker's, grip.

The left hand is turned too far over the grip with too many knuckles showing, the 'V' pointing outside the player's chin and right shoulder. The right hand is too much on the underside of the grip which lies in the palm of the hand. Unless a conscious effort is made to open the face on the backswing, the club face travels away from the ball in a closed position and remains closed when the wrists set.

At the top of the backswing the club face points towards the sky. During the downswing the dominant right hand cannot be subdued and it starts to square the club face prematurely, closing it before impact. Although this can be avoided with great effort, by resisting the natural forces in the swing, it will not maximize your full potential with the driver.

Aiming right of the target

A common reaction in an attempt to counteract the hook is to aim to the right of the target. This often has a reverse effect and can actually increase the problem. The player knows that to bring the ball back on target the hands now have to produce a hook. This conscious effort produces an even quicker hand action exaggerating the hooked ball flight beyond control.

Left: The right hand can over-dominate and close the club face at impact. Above: Aiming right to counteract the problem may cause the hands to work excessively and close the face even more.

Swing faults

Standing too far from the ball

Standing too far from the ball, or poor posture, encourages the swing path to travel inside the line too early, thereby positioning the club on a flat swing plane. This can lead to a reverse pivot which positions the club across the line at the top. As the hands and arms travel from inside the line, the right hip often blocks their passage, promoting excessive hand action to release the club head.

Left and below: Reaching at address encourages an early inside path leading to a reverse pivot and positioning the club across the line at the top. As the club travels from the inside, it promotes excessive hand action.

Building the correct grip

Many players set up and grip the club correctly yet simply close the face during the takeaway which, unless compensated for in the downswing, will close the face at impact. Returning the club face consistently square at impact can only be achieved from an orthodox grip.

Good posture

Notice the angle formed between the club shaft and trunk when you set up; this is achieved through flexing, not bending, the knees, and bending from the waist to ground the club. As the hands and arms start the club away from the ball the left side of the body

Above: The left hand controls a gradual recovery, returning the club head from inside back on to the target line at impact.

commences a pivotal turn; in unison with this turn the club face position alters gradually until the hands are in a position to commence the wrist set process, which works in unison with the body turn and arm swing. At the top of

the backswing the shaft is on line with the club face in the square or neutral position.

As the weight begins to transfer and the body starts to unwind, the club travels down on an inside path from where the hands can effect a controlled recovery to square the club face at impact. If you look closely at what happens in the downswing, you can see that the club face is in an ever changing position. Just before impact it is slightly open; at impact, and momentarily through impact, it is square to the target and travelling on the target line before it

Below: The club face angle is continually in transition: open just prior to impact, square at impact, and progressively closing after impact.

begins to close as the club head path travels inside the line. Initially if you begin to slice, do not worry you will be close to correct delivery. During practice swings monitor the transition of the club face position.

Swing faults

Slicing

Many of the faults that lead to slicing are caused through problems at address. Standing too erect or too close to the ball promotes a poor start to the swing. This type of set up can lead to a lateral movement during the takeaway, where the hips slide the weight on to the right top, throwing the club on an outside downswing path and causing it to travel across the ball and inside the target line through impact. In an acute case the

Above: Standing too close can lead to a sequence of poor movements. Right: The hips slide laterally, and the left shoulder tilts, forcing the arms to lift the club into an upright position.

Above right: The right side comes over the top forcing the swing path to travel from outside to inside. The heel of the club may even contact the ball first. Right: A slice may occur when feet, knees, hips and shoulders point to the left in the set up.

leg, and the left shoulder tilts steeply under the chin, forcing the arms to lift the club into a steep upright plane.

From this position, correct weight transference cannot be made, and the right side of the body comes over the

right side comes so much over the top that the ball is hit off the heel of the club.

Failure to understand the concept of target alignment and to follow a pre-shot routine can result in an open set up where the feet, hips and shoulders aim left of the target. This will promote a club head path on takeaway which travels outside the line with the club shaft left of the target at the top of the backswing. On the downswing the club follows a similar path and travels inside the target line through impact.

Above: The club head starts outside the target line and the shaft aims left at the top. The shoulders open too early in the downswing forcing an out-to-in path.

A weak grip

This is when the left hand is positioned too much on top of the shaft with the right hand wrapped too far over, and both 'V's point more towards the player's chin; this usually encourages open shoulder alignment and is a common cause of slicing. At the start of the swing the right hand rolls the club face open with the toe of the club pointing directly at the ground at the top of

Above: A weak grip can influence the hands and roll the club face excessively open at the takeaway.

the backswing. Quite often a player with a weak grip who rolls the face open does achieve a reasonable swing plane at the top, although the ability to effect a gradual squaring of the club face cannot be achieved consistently.

Swing faults

The correct set up

Reaching for the ball at address makes it very difficult to maintain an inside path on the downswing; the player's weight often falls towards the toes, promoting an acute out-to-in path which makes a glancing contact from the toe at impact. If the ball is positioned too far forward in the stance, the club head path may be travelling inside the line as contact is made.

If you position the left hand correctly on the grip, the right hand can then be applied correctly. The key at first is to use a two-stage routine that

Above and right: Reaching can position too much weight on the toes at address and this can shift back on to the heels during the backswing and then return to the toes, forcing the right side to spin out and contacting the ball on the toe.

ensures correct placement. It is important to stabilize the club by holding it between your thumb and forefinger (right hand). As you position the left, make sure that it is turned sufficiently to show at least two knuckles; this will ensure that the 'V' points between your chin and right shoulder. From the player's view looking down, the thumb is positioned to the right centre of the grip. Position the grip in the fingers of the right hand which allows the closed pad to sit over the left thumb, both 'V's pointing between the chin and right shoulder.

Right: Stand erect with knees slightly flexed. Bend slowly forward from the waist to ground the club. A right angle should be formed between the shaft and your trunk. The centre of gravity should be in the lower legs towards the toes.

Practice drill

Work on your new set up in front of a mirror. Stand side-on to the mirror, erect with arms extended and the club shaft parallel with the ground. Slowly bend forwards from your waist until the club is grounded. It is important that you feel the centre of gravity positioned down towards your calves and through to the balls of the feet. The reflection in the mirror should give the impression of the shaft of the club and your trunk forming a 'T', or right angle. This helps promote the correct turning motion.

Swing faults

Pre-shot routine

You can cure the problem of ball position and alignment by adopting a simple pre-shot routine (see page 119).

Practice drill

Although your improved posture will promote a good turn, you should practise this pivotal move by placing a club behind your back. The club on the ground is used as a reference point for your

swing centre or axis. Slowly rotate the left side of your body around the axis/centre until the club behind your back is parallel with the club on the ground.

Swing path check

To familiarize yourself with correct club face control and swing path, place some tape or a club on the ground as a reference point for your target line. At first, make numerous practice swings, if possible in front of a mirror; this will enable you to observe and feel the correct movements.

With improved set up, your hands and arms will start in unison with the turning motion; the club head starts

away on the target line and travels inside as the turn progresses. This also alters the club face position gradually. As the turn and backswing are completed, you will have an ideal club face and shaft position at the top.

On the downswing, feel the left side of your body lead the weight transfer, with the left hand pulling the club down to maintain an inside path. Your grip will allow you to control the uncocking of the wrists, and square the club face as the club head travels from inside on to the target line.

Above left and above: From a good set up and posture, the club starts on the target line, gradually travelling inside it. At waist height and at the top, the club face is square and the club shaft is aiming parallel with the target line.

Practice drill

Simulate your grip to practise hand and arm control. Gradually rotate the club face (back of gloved left hand) and then return it to impact. This will train your hands to better control the swing path and club face position in the vital last part of the downswing.

CHAPTER TEN

Practice

Jim Christine

Practice is an essential ingredient in becoming a better player. No-one has ever shown sustained improvement without it. In my experience, the players who work hardest on the practice fairway are the best players. Now that you know what you should be doing, practising is the only way to introduce these skills into your game of golf.

Every golf coach has heard the excuse, 'I didn't have time to practise'. Well, if that is the case, it is very difficult to improve. It may be very difficult to make enough time to go to a golf range; that is understandable. However, all I am going to ask you for is five minutes: five minutes three times a day. The following drills do not require ball hitting, so you can do them at home, in the office or in the garden. You have no excuse now: give them some time and you will certainly improve your driving.

Practice

Pivot for power

1 Build your coil

Take up the body pivot exercise position shown. If you are indoors, stand in a door frame as a substitute for the shafts.

Start turning smoothly, concentrating on moving your right hip and shoulder around and behind you. Make sure that your body weight is shifting gradually more on to your right foot. Do not allow any swaying motion; make sure that you do not bump onto the shaft on the right side of your body! At the top your shoulders should have turned through 90 degrees from your starting position, and you should feel that your body weight has moved back towards the heel of your right foot. Bounce on your right knee a little, and feel how that slightly reduces your hip turn, then turn your shoulders a little further. You should feel a slight stretching in the big muscles across your back and in your right thigh. This is coil! Relax, then bounce your right knee again. Repeat three times.

2 Set for power

From the photo (opposite right), start to turn back to the left with the whole of your left side. Feel your body weight shifting back towards your left foot until you reach the position shown below. Your left knee and hip have just touched the shaft to the left of your body. Your knees and hips are now in line with the two shafts, while your shoulders are still pointing slightly to the right. Your body

weight should be distributed evenly between your feet. Try to feel as though you are pushing your weight down into the ground, squatting slightly, pushing your knees a little

apart. You are now set to deliver your power through impact. Repeat the set three times.

3 Rotate to accelerate

Rotate your left side around behind you as fast as you can until you reach the position shown below. Make sure that you do not knock over that right-hand shaft, and keep your balance. Work on increasing your speed of rotation, but keep control of your finish. Repeat this acceleration three times. This is a complex exercise; two repetitions of the full exercise will take you five minutes.

Practice

Get familiar

Many people do not know their driver well! It may be that you have not used it much in the past, or that you have only just bought it. You need to get to know it, and this provides a perfect opportunity to practise your grip also.

Leave your driver around the house, in a spot where you will often pass by it. Each time you pass it, pick it up! Position your hands on the grip in their correct position, and give the club a little waggle; it takes less than one minute! Drill number one, but do not forget to take your club with you when you go out to play!

Mirror mirror

Practise your set up in front of the mirror or a window where you can see your reflection. Work into position, check your alignment, get those lines parallel, check your posture; make it look good! It is a good idea to stick a picture of a top player in his set-up position on to your mirror. Make your position look as good as his. Only another minute: take your set up five times.

Build your leverage

From your set-up position, slowly move back by turning your right hip and shoulder. Allow your right elbow to fold and your wrists to set until your left arm is horizontal to the ground. At this stage, the club shaft must be at right angles to your left forearm. Repeat this drill five times.

Hold the leverage

From the top of your backswing, move your body weight smoothly back towards your left foot. Practise holding the angle created between your left arm and the club shaft at the top of your backswing until you reach the position shown far right. Do not exaggerate this move – just hold the angle from the top to the position shown. This is quite a strenuous exercise; you should repeat it three times.

Stretch for power

Take up your set-up position for a normal swing. Move your right hand down until it is at the bottom of the grip. Your left hand must stay in its normal position, creating a gap of some three to four inches between your two hands. Turn your right side back into a normal backswing and, as you reach the end of your movement, you should feel the big muscles across your back stretching a little. Take it easy, do not pull any of these, but see if you can make a full movement as shown. Again, this is hard work. Repeat the exercise three times.

Practice

The swish drill: release the club

Take up your full set-up position, and then just raise the club head a little off the ground. You are going to use your full swing action here, turning into your right side and through to your left. Accelerate the club on the forward swing, and swish it through the air in front of your body. Smoothly build up as much acceleration as you can while still maintaining your balanced finishing position. Imagine that you are turning to the right to throw your golf club straight down the fairway as you move through to the left! Then imagine that you are going to let your club go and release it for maximum swish. Make sure the swish takes place in front of your body in your impact zone. That swish is club head speed which will eventually move the ball a long way. Repeat 10 times and this will give you the feeling of the swing you should be using on the course.

Pivot for control

Imagine the shafts that you can see to the left and right of the body in these photos are acting like a stall around your body. Practise your body pivot, making sure that you transfer your weight back into your right side while staying within your stall.

Move your weight back to the left, just touching the side of your stall with your left hip and knee. Turn your left side behind you to stay within your stall at the finish. Make sure that your body weight is almost entirely on your left foot at the finish, but do not crash out of your stall. Repeat five times.

Practice

Maintain the spine angle

You are back in front of your mirror again, but this time as if you were hitting the ball directly away from the mirror. Assume the body pivot position shown and practise your movement, making sure that your spine angle remains constant.

The position shown below (right) is common but a total disaster.

The spine angle has increased, tilting the shoulders and straightening the right knee. Do not let this happen to you! Follow the sequence shown; the spine angle remains constant through the movement until the ball is well on its way, and it is permissible to stand up a little, thereby reducing strain on your spine. Repeat five times.

Create the arc

In the photographs, the right hand has taken up an underhand grasp of the left wrist, just where your watch-strap would be if you wear your watch on the left wrist. From this position, practise your backswing, keeping your left arm comfortably extended. Do not lock your left elbow, but just keep your left arm extended. As you can see, it looks slightly bowed – this is correct arm tension. Practise your backswing arc 10 times.

Practice

Build the impact

Although you must realise that impact is not a position, it is very important to train your muscles to appreciate just what the ideal impact should be. The photo below shows the correct body position: 60 per cent of your body weight should now be on your left foot, and your right heel is just beginning to come off the ground. A line drawn across your hips should point 20 to 30 degrees left of their set-up position, and a line across your shoulders 5 to 10 degrees left of their starting position. Your head should be inclined to the right slightly, making sure that your eyes are looking at the back of the ball. Position your left arm so that it is comfortably extended; your left hand should be opposite the middle of

your left thigh, a little further forward than its set-up position. Your right arm comes into the picture now. Make sure that there is still a little of the angle left in your right elbow and wrist. Look how correct it all is when the club is taken into this position. If you pass through impact like this, you will be a great driver. Build your impact piece by piece five times.

Practice

Link the movement

Look at the exercise photographic sequence shown. As you take up the position shown below, you will feel a slight pressure between your chest, your right hand, and your left arm.

Take a small backswing, turning your right side into the movement.

Check that your left arm moves in unison, and maintain the same pressure between your arm, hand and body as you move into the position below. Start moving back towards

impact, making sure that you are moving as a unit by maintaining the same pressure through impact and into the position below (right). You should have experienced no change in pressure in this movement so far, no increase or decrease. Now allow your left arm to move smoothly away from your body until you finish in the position shown. As you can see, your left hand should finish just above the level of the top of your head, and your left upper arm is a continuation of your shoulder line.

Practice

Right arm link movement

Repeat the previous exercise for your right arm. Look at the sequence, and try to maintain the pressure in the same way as in your left arm exercise. You will feel your right elbow and wrist both flex slightly to allow you to hold the pressure, and the sensation from the position below to that opposite (left) should be such that your arm slides up over your hand to

its finishing position. In these photos, your right elbow should be relaxed with your hand level with the top of your head. Repeat these exercises five times, linking your movement to a well-balanced finish: a sure sign that all is well in your golf swing.

Practice

How good are you?

A final exercise: place two white tees in the ground about six inches apart, so that your club can just pass between them. Take up your set up with your club between the tees. Make a free swing, the one you are going to use on the course. Turn back and accelerate through to your

finish. Are your tees still there? Repeat this free swing 10 times. You should not hit any tees! Keep a score of the number of times you manage to swing without hitting the tees.

Summary

These practice exercises and drills prepare you to swing well and play well on the course. They are not for thinking about while you are playing: they are for practising between your games of golf. Choose some different ones every day, practise for five minutes three times a day, and you will certainly improve. When you go to the course, think only of turning back and accelerating through to a finish. In the seconds it takes to hit a full drive, you do not have the time to think about any more. It is all too easy to try too hard, think about it too much, and destroy all the good work you have done. Keep your mind clear, let your swing work freely, and above all enjoy those long, straight drives.

CHAPTER ELEVEN

Left-handers

Tony Moore

There have been few top class left-handed golfers. Bob Charles, the New Zealander, now playing exquisite golf on the Seniors' Tour, springs to mind as being perhaps the best of all the recent left-handers. Why should this be the case? Is it that those who are left-handed do not take up golf? Not at all. There are many left-handed amateur golfers playing week in and week out but they are far out-numbered by the right-handed. This in itself brings many problems for the left-hander.

● Golf courses are almost always set up with the right-hander in mind and this may cause some problems in course strategy for the left-handed slicer or hooker.

● Most general golf shops store little in the way of left-handed equipment, thus making the choice of goods limited.

● Golf instruction books and videos are usually made for the right-hander.

It is often a good idea, therefore, for people who are left-handed at most things to try to play golf right-handed in the first instance. This is one option that would certainly help with club selection. Some people can even play golf both right-handed and left-handed. The former England cricket captain Brian Close apparently plays golf both ways – he is even single figure handicap right-handed and left-handed. However, if you decide to play golf left-handed, here are some tips that may help.

Left-handers

Gripping the club

Most instruction books and videos cater for the right-hander and the description of where to put the hands often revolves around 'right hand and left hand'. You may use these forms of instruction but instead of thinking about right hands and left hands, simply read the book and translate right hand into 'top hand' and left hand into 'bottom hand'. All the principles about selecting a method of holding the club are the same: most people who have medium or large hands could use the overlap method, whereas golfers with short fingers should use an interlocking grip.

In the overlap grip, the left-handed golfer will have the little finger of the left hand (the bottom hand) placed either on top of the index finger of the right hand (the top hand) or in the gap between the index finger and second finger. To form the interlocking grip, this time the little finger of the bottom hand and the index finger of the top

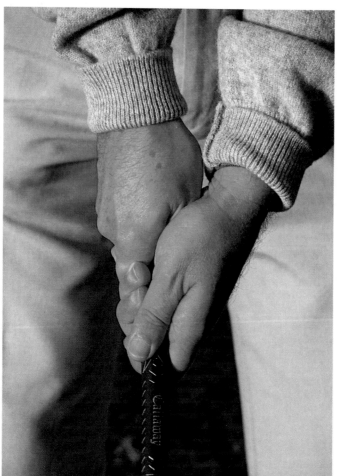

Left and above: These photographs show the left-handed version of the Vardon, or overlapping, grip. Notice how the left hand is on the bottom.

hand interlock. In all cases, the top hand is the right hand. The baseball grip may also be used by some left-handed golfers, particularly if you have small fingers. You should read Chapter 2 in this book to learn how to hold the club properly; for the left-handed golfer, translating, as mentioned before, right hand into top hand and left hand into bottom hand will help.

Right: This photograph shows the interlocking grip for a left-hander. Again, the left hand is the 'bottom' hand with the right hand on top.

Teeing-up

Problems arise for left-handers as soon as they reach the tee box. First of all, look for an area on the tee box that allows you to tee up the ball on some short, flat grass. Check also that the ground where you place your feet in the stance is also the best available. Often in adverse weather and particularly in winter, the left-hander has to tee up in the places where all the right-handed golfers have been standing, and consequently this area may be 'spiked up' and muddy.

For left-handed golfers, this situation has become increasingly common, due to the often considerable demand on the tee box, that some courses use tee mats, but these are particularly unpleasant for the left-hander as most of the wear and tear on an old mat is just where you want to put the ball. Poorly supported tee mats can also bend and become bumpy where the right-hander stands, leaving the left-hander a muddy, curled up, uneven surface from which to tee off. On the tee (and only on the tee) you are able of course to flatten, clean and improve the ground behind your ball, but even this practice sometimes provides insufficient assistance. You are allowed in the Rules to move the ball backwards from the line of the tee markers for a maximum of two club lengths. With the driver this is quite a long way, and even on the worst tee box, you should be able to find somewhere reasonable to tee up. Care must always be taken to select the best part of the tee box available to you in order to get maximum benefit from your shot. I suggest that the left-hander pays particular attention to this.

Left-handers

Aligning the club to play a shot

You may use the following method to take up your stance and align the club face so that you can direct the ball at your intended target.

1 Once you have teed up, stand three or so yards (nine feet, approximately three metres) behind the ball and try to visualize the shot that you intend to play, looking in particular at where you would like the ball to land and then stop.

2 Pick a point about two feet in front of the ball which is directly between the ball and your target. This may be a clump of grass, a mark on the ground, maybe even a daisy, anything that you can remember as being the point on your target line.

Right: Visualize your intended shot, standing three yards behind the ball. Far right: The point you pick in front of the ball is represented by the tee peg in the photo

3 Take up your grip and then put the club face on the ground behind the ball (taking care not to knock it off; this is irritating and breaks concentration even though it is not a penalty at this stage). Square up the club face so that it aims at your selected point. The next stage is to align your feet and position yourself in such a way that your arms are in a comfortable position away from your body in order for you to make a swing.

4 Imagine a line that runs parallel with your target-aim point-ball and extends backwards about one yard through your ball. Your feet should be placed so that your toes are on this imaginary line – this ensures that both the club face, your feet, your hips and your shoulders are parallel to where you intend to hit the ball. When practising, you may use

With regard to ball position at address, when using the driver a simple tip for the left-hander is to make sure that the ball is positioned opposite the right heel. This set up is clearly shown in the photograph below.

Far left: Instead of imagining a line that runs parallel with your target-aim point-ball, you can use a club as shown here to help you align correctly.

a real line to help you align correctly and there are some pieces of equipment available that assist you with this, although these techniques may not be used on the course.

Obviously the grip and your swing path will also determine the direction in which the golf ball will travel, but correct alignment is most important and this is often the cause of a shot that is hit straight but misses the target area.

The swing

The principles of swinging the golf club are the same, whether you play right-handed or left-handed. You should try to get your hands, arms and shoulders working together to form a rhythmic, athletic swing. All the principles previously described in this book may be used by the left-hander.

Left-handers

Course strategy

I have already mentioned that golf courses tend to be set up for right-handed golfers. You might be wondering why this may be the case. The following examples demonstrate some of the pit-falls for a left-hander.

Fairway bunkers

You will see that this hole has a bunker strategically positioned for the shorter sliced shot and the longer hooked shot – for right-handers. Left-handers will hook and slice their bad shots to different positions. In this case the hole favours the left-handed golfer, but in some cases the situation will be reversed.

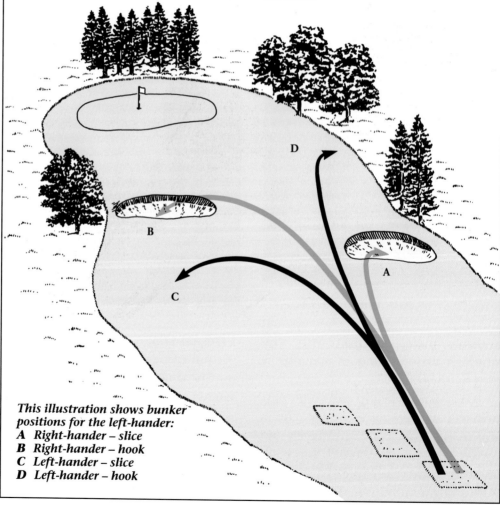

This illustration shows bunker positions for the left-hander:
A *Right-hander – slice*
B *Right-hander – hook*
C *Left-hander – slice*
D *Left-hander – hook*

Right hand dog-leg

In the situation below, the hole is a dog-leg to the right. This is a common design on many golf courses. Suppose that the hole is a par four and our left-handed golfer is a slicer. The ball travels shorter distances when sliced and this will cause this golfer great difficulty in reaching the green with the second shot. The left-handed hooker will have even more problems hitting out of the trees on the right! For the right-handed hooker, the hole is made much easier, and the extra length gained gives rise to a shorter shot into the green. One consolation is that the right-handed slicer will also have problems on this hole!

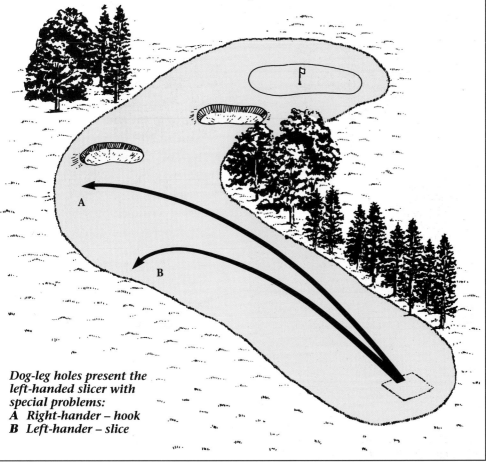

Dog-leg holes present the left-handed slicer with special problems:
A *Right-hander – hook*
B *Left-hander – slice*

Therefore, it is preferable to avoid any problems, and left-handed golfers should try to develop a good swing that enables them to hit shots straight and consistently, thereby minimizing some problems encountered on the course.

Left-handers

Equipment selection

All the principles behind selecting the equipment that suits you best, described by Jim Christine earlier in this book, apply to the left-handed golfer. Your choice may be more restricted in the smaller golf shop but a good professional's shop will have some of the more popular metal and wooden drivers and if your choice is not in stock they may be ordered. Some professionals make customized golf clubs and the left-hander will not be at a disadvantage if this course of action is followed. Most golf shops carry golf gloves for the left-hander, and these, of course, are worn on the right hand. In general, a golf professional who knows he has left-handers in the club will make sure that they are properly catered for.

Instruction

You may feel that your local golf professional, if he is right-handed, is unable to teach you, but this is far from the truth. The fundamental principles of the golf swing, teeing up, grip and alignment, are exactly the same. Problem solving is also easy and all PGA Qualified Professionals will be able to help you with your game.

Summary

To conclude, the left-handed golfer has a number of problems when playing golf, usually not experienced by the right-hander. However, if you take more care and attention when teeing up and aligning your shots, and apply more thought in your course strategy you will soon improve your driving and also lower your scores. Good luck!

Index

Golf books from HarperCollins*Publishers*